Cambridge Elements

Elements in Religion in Late Antiquity
edited by
Andrew S. Jacobs
Harvard Divinity School

ISRAEL AND ITS HEIRS IN LATE ANTIQUITY

Andrew Tobolowsky
The College of William & Mary

Shaftesbury Road, Cambridge CB2 8EA, United Kingdom

One Liberty Plaza, 20th Floor, New York, NY 10006, USA

477 Williamstown Road, Port Melbourne, VIC 3207, Australia

314–321, 3rd Floor, Plot 3, Splendor Forum, Jasola District Centre, New Delhi – 110025, India

103 Penang Road, #05–06/07, Visioncrest Commercial, Singapore 238467

Cambridge University Press is part of Cambridge University Press & Assessment, a department of the University of Cambridge.

We share the University's mission to contribute to society through the pursuit of education, learning and research at the highest international levels of excellence.

www.cambridge.org
Information on this title: www.cambridge.org/9781009598668

DOI: 10.1017/9781009392891

© Andrew Tobolowsky 2025

This publication is in copyright. Subject to statutory exception and to the provisions of relevant collective licensing agreements, no reproduction of any part may take place without the written permission of Cambridge University Press & Assessment.

When citing this work, please include a reference to the DOI 10.1017/9781009392891

First published 2025

A catalogue record for this publication is available from the British Library

ISBN 978-1-009-59866-8 Hardback
ISBN 978-1-009-39291-4 Paperback
ISSN 2633-8602 (online)
ISSN 2633-8599 (print)

Cambridge University Press & Assessment has no responsibility for the persistence or accuracy of URLs for external or third-party internet websites referred to in this publication and does not guarantee that any content on such websites is, or will remain, accurate or appropriate.

For EU product safety concerns, contact us at Calle de José Abascal, 56, 1°, 28003 Madrid, Spain, or email eugpsr@cambridge.org

Israel and Its Heirs in Late Antiquity

Elements in Religion in Late Antiquity

DOI: 10.1017/9781009392891
First published online: April 2025

Andrew Tobolowsky
The College of William & Mary

Author for correspondence: Andrew Tobolowsky, abtobolowsky@wm.edu

Abstract: This Element explores constructions of Israelite identity among Jewish, Samaritan Israelites, and Christian authors in Late Antiquity, especially early Late Antiquity. It identifies three major strategies for claiming an Israelite identity between these three groups: a "biological" strategy, a "biology plus" strategy, and an "abiological" strategy, referring to the difference between Jewish claims to Israel premised on exclusive biological descent, Samaritan Israelite acknowledgments of shared descent, and the "Verus Israel" tradition in Christianity, which disavows the importance of descent. Using this framework, it makes various general conclusions about the construction of ethnic identity itself, including the inadequacy of treating descent claims as the sine qua non of ethnicity and role played in any given vision of ethnic identity by the individual creativity of a given author.

Keywords: Late Antiquity, early Judaism, early Christianity, Samaritans, ethnicity

© Andrew Tobolowsky 2025

ISBNs: 9781009598668 (HB), 9781009392914 (PB), 9781009392891 (OC)
ISSNs: 2633-8602 (online), 2633-8599 (print)

Contents

Introduction 1

Jewish Constructions of Israelite Identity in Late Antiquity 5

Samaritan Israelite Constructions of Israelite Identity
in Late Antiquity 22

Christian Constructions of Israelite Identity
in Late Antiquity 34

Conclusion 52

Bibliography 58

Introduction

This little study you hold in your hands, or, as it may be, view on your screen marks my second attempt to map a "world full of Israels."[1] The first, a book called *The Myth of the Twelve Tribes of Israel* offered a whirlwind tour, a survey of a fascinating and still much neglected phenomenon: the presence for thousands of years now of many different groups, all around the world, who identify as the people Israel. On this return trip, I intend a more leisurely pace focusing narrowly on the competition over the identity and legacy of Israel between Jews, Samaritan Israelites, and Christians, specifically in the era known to scholars as Late Antiquity, generally defined as a period that began around the turn of the third century CE and continued into the seventh or eighth.[2] Indeed, within that span, I will largely focus on the first half, and on that level the project of this piece is, if not simple, then at least straightforward.

Yet the first book was not only about Israels but about the phenomenon of ethnic identity itself.[3] One important point I wanted to make is that the mere *existence* of so many different groups identifying as the "same" group, quite independently of each other, is more of a challenge to typical ways of thinking about ethnic identity than many realize, which is to say, as unique groups with particular and well-defined characteristics.[4] Similarly, and more to the point of this study, I think we tend to imagine ethnic groups building their identities around a single, cherished repertoire of traditions that is specifically and intrinsically theirs, passed down through the generations, and that if they refashion themselves, it is largely by telling *these* stories in new ways. But here we see a wide variety of groups adopting, as I say, the same identity, using the same traditions *as each other*, and traditions that were also neither theirs originally nor uniquely theirs in any sense at all. Instead, they are traditions that were once the special property of the ancient Israelites and Judahites alone, now appearing in a book that is, to some extent, the common property of many groups: the Hebrew Bible.[5] And if the members of a group, or different groups, can go to bed thinking

---

[1] Tobolowsky, *The Myth of the Twelve Tribes of Israel*, 2.
[2] For the debate about the contours of Late Antiquity see the lucid discussion in James, "The Rise and Function of the Concept," 20–21. See also Brown, *The World of Late Antiquity*; Brown, *Late Antiquity*; Bowersock, Brown, and Grabar, eds., *Late Antiquity*.
[3] My views on the topic of ethnicity, expressed more extensively below, have been particularly shaped by the work of Andreas Wimmer, Rogers Brubaker, and Patrick J. Geary, for which see particularly Wimmer, "The Making and Unmaking of Ethnic Boundaries," 970–1022; Wimmer, "Herder's Heritage," 244–70; Brubaker, *Ethnicity without Groups*; Brubaker, *Nationalist Politics*; Geary, *The Myth of Nations*.
[4] That is, we tend to think of ethnic groups as defined by their differences from all others.
[5] As I observed about the early Mormons, who were mainly of Anglo-Protestant ancestry, "[i]n other words, if, say a future Mormon had joined another famous New York resident, Rip Van Winkle, for a nap in 1819 (the year Washington Irving's book was published, though it is set in an

of themselves as one thing, and wake up thinking of themselves as Israelites, and use traditions that are not "theirs," maybe a lot more is possible, as far as ethnic phenomena are concerned, than we often suppose.

Indeed, it turns out that "becoming Israel" is by no means an otherwise unexampled phenomenon.[6] In the ancient world, and even into the medieval period, there were a number of different individuals and groups who all claimed descent from the heroes of the Trojan War. Stories that make this claim include the *Aeneid*, a Roman story about Trojan founders.[7] And I understand that, even in more recent periods, Nazi ideology stressed a strong connection between Nazi Germany and various classical forebears, especially ancient Greece.[8] In breadth, depth, and historical duration, however, "becoming Israel" is indeed unique and as a result offers a unique opportunity to learn something new about ethnic identity itself. Certainly, in studying how so many different groups construct the "same" identity from the "same" traditions in different times and places, we can learn a lot about how many different shapes the same identity can really take and how many different things the same traditions can really be used to do.

If in the first book I was primarily interested in *how* one set of traditions could be used as the starting point for so many different versions of Israelite identity, however, in this one my focus is on the nature of the relationship between those who construct visions of ethnicity and the traditions they construct them from. In other words, now that we know that an author can build ethnicities from a wider range of traditions than we might suppose, we turn our attention to all that an author can do from the traditions they select, after they select them. Then, just as a global survey served the needs of the prior study, the context of inter-ethnic competition is what is most useful here, because it so multiplies the opportunities to study the use of inherited traditions in ethnic boundary-making activity.

Basically, then, what we will see in this Element is that there is no one way to use an inherited set of traditions to construct a vision of ethnic boundaries. More than that, there is no such thing as an "ethnic identity" that stands *apart* from how it is being constructed in a given case. There is no essential content to an ethnic identity, no one thing that it has to be. Ethnicity is a particular way of using inherited traditions to describe the difference between a group and other groups, but the imperative to define is a far more important part of the equation than any one way of doing it. A person constructing a vision of the ethnic group

---

earlier period), he or she would have fallen asleep a Gentile and woken up an Israelite" (Tobolowsky, *The Myth of the Twelve Tribes of Israel*, 184–85).

[6] Tobolowsky, *The Myth of the Twelve Tribes of Israel*, 1–21.
[7] Malkin, *The Returns of Odysseus*.   [8] See Chapoutot, *Greeks, Romans, Germans*.

by telling a story about the past or relying on the authority of inherited understandings in other ways can do whatever seems best to them to do as an individual. And within the context of their effort, ethnicity is really whatever they say it is.

To be clear, these conclusions are not unique to this study, however little impact they may yet have had on many studies of ancient ethnicity to date.[9] I count among my guiding lights the observation of James C. Miller that "the ongoing process of boundary definition and maintenance *is* ethnicity" and of Judith Lieu that, in constructing identities, "the same history can be used differently by different claimants, while different histories may be reconciled with each other in a single text or author."[10] Even more centrally, my conclusions here are strongly influenced by the work of Denise Buell, who, in a study of early constructions of Christian identity has also argued that ethnicity is not a fixed point but the very tension between "fixity" and "fluidity" that we see in any given example of its actual construction.[11]

Above all, I am drawing on Buell's argument that even the essential contents of an ethnic identity are up for grabs depending on who is doing the defining. In other words, in scholarship today, it is still generally assumed that for an identity articulation to be ethnic in nature, it must include a tradition of shared descent.[12] Just as with "our own" stories versus the stories of others, however, it actually seems clear from the evidence that while what I will call "biological" constructions of ethnic identity are *common*, that does not mean that they are *required*.[13] Instead, claiming exclusive biological descent turns out to be only one way of constructing ethnic boundaries. And once again, the unique opportunity afforded by the presence of multiple groups constructing the same identity in different ways will help make this point clearer than it would be otherwise. Just as an example, the Christian tradition that I am most interested in is the so-called "Verus Israel" tradition, in which various authors made the case that they were the "true Israel" explicitly in spite of the fact that they were not the biological

---

[9] Even today, for example, as Carly L. Crouch observes, "[t]he primordialist framework ... is probably the form of ethnic identity which has most frequently found its way into discussions of biblical texts" (Crouch, *The Making of Israel*, 99).

[10] Miller, "Ethnicity and the Hebrew Bible," 173; Lieu, *Christian Identity*, 97.

[11] Buell, *Why This New Race*, 7. Buell herself cites as a major influence the work of Ann Laura Stoler (Stoler, "Racial Histories," 183–206).

[12] As she puts it, "[t]he majority opinion about ethnicity from anthropology and sociologists, as well as by other scholars who draw upon their work, is that ethnicity entails claims of common kinship or descent from a common group or ancestor. That is, such claims are generally viewed as a necessary criterion of ethnicity – if we find these claims, we might have 'ethnicity'; if we do not, then we do not have ethnicity." Buell, *Why This New Race*, 9. Examples of influential definitions in this vein can be found in the work of Anthony Smith and Jonathan M. Hall (Smith, *The Ethnic Origins of Nations*, 24; Hall, *Ethnic Identity in Greek Antiquity*, 25).

[13] Buell, *Why This New Race*, 9.

descendants of the original Israelites. Other than that, however, these authors were constructing the same identity as the Jews and Samaritan Israelites I will discuss here, using many of the same traditions, in roughly the same time and place. If we wanted to argue that two of these Israels were ethnic in nature, but the third was not, on what grounds could we make the case? Such is the value of comparison.

Thus, in what follows, I will not focus on what the contents of ethnic identities must be but instead on the crucial question of all that may be done *with* an – or any – inherited set of contents. And to that end, I will organize my discussion around three of what I will refer to as ethnic "strategies," which were executed in each case in a great many different ways. This will help us get a sense of how much variation can exist, even in the operation of overarching concepts that can seem, from afar, like stable expressions of what ethnicity is. In the Jewish case, where I will focus especially though not exclusively on the Babylonian Talmud, I will identify a "biological" strategy of claiming to be the only true heirs of Israel by virtue of exclusive biological descent. In the Samaritan Israelite case, I will discuss the operation of what I will call a "biology plus" strategy, which is to say that Samaritan Israelite authors seem generally to have acknowledged that they shared descent with the Jewish people but claimed superiority anyway, on the basis of superior scriptures, practices, and beliefs. And in the Christian case, I will focus on the proponents of "Verus Israel" just mentioned, who claimed to be the people Israel without possessing biological descent. Naturally, I will call this the "abiological" strategy. But I will also show how much variety there is in the deployment of each strategy, within each context. And in all but the Samaritan Israelite case, I will also be able to show that even these grand strategies were only one among a number thereof that operated in Late Antique contexts within the same groups.

These discussions will certainly help confirm the view that constructing ethnic identity as a product of biological descent is *just* a strategy, rather than the fundamental basis of ethnicity. But they will also illustrate the more central point. Ethnicity is not a stable inheritance, existing in multiple variations; it *is* variation. There is no objectively definable abstraction that we can call ethnicity from which the versions of identity that exist proceed. Instead, inherited ideas about what the ethnic group consists of are part of the building blocks from which actual ethnic articulations are made, and individual ways of building ethnicity are almost infinitely variable. And this is the case especially because an individual author can do far more with an inheritance – with, in fact, multiple different inheritances – than more conservative models of ethnic identity suppose. The nature of the relationship between those who construct ethnic identities and the traditions they construct them from is determined, most of all, by what the shapers want what they shape to accomplish not only in terms of the real and perceived needs of a given social context but by genuinely *individual* apprehensions and idiosyncrasies.

Jewish Constructions of Israelite Identity in Late Antiquity

We might usefully think of ethnicity in terms of starting points, and what happens next. Well before Late Antiquity began, this dynamic was clearly visible in post-biblical, Jewish constructions of Israelite identity. Jason Staples has offered an illuminating look at it, referring as well to the *complexity* of interactions between "present people" and traditions. His way of putting it is that certain ideas were "unavoidably in the air for those socialized into this environment" but their expression in "authoritative texts" was combined with "commemorative rituals (e.g. Passover)" to reinvent those ideas in various ways – and differently for different authors.[14] Well beyond ritual, the capacity of reinvention is a constant and needs nothing more than an individual's idiosyncratic apprehensions of what a tradition should mean and could do. Those apprehensions were, of course, also shaped by daily experiences, subjectivities, and rhetorical partners, often below the level of what we can now reconstruct at this distance, but they also remain stubbornly individual.

So, for example, Staples describes a crucial difference between how the first-century Jewish historian Josephus represents the Israelite past that all Israel is heir to and how certain other early Jewish authors do. Specifically, Josephus – in his account of what he regarded as Jewish history, which stretches back to the beginning of the biblical vision thereof – shows a keen awareness of the difference between the kingdoms of Judah and Israel. He consistently distinguishes in his work between the terms "Ioudaioi" and "Israelite," correctly recognizing that the Judahite people, rather than the people of both kingdoms, are the historically accurate Ioudaioi, which is to say, the Jews.[15] Then, Josephus uses Israelite for the most part to mean "specifically ... those of the northern kingdom" and prefers Hebraios to Israelite for the ancestors of both Israel and Judah, which others regard as "all Israel."[16]

Meanwhile, even in that same period, there were indeed authors who chose to elide the historical distinction between Judah and Israel in referring back to the same past, in order to emphasize the central importance of "all Israel" instead.

---

[14] Staples, *The Idea of Israel*, 6. "In other words, a received 'narrative substructure' and the rhetorical and descriptive lexicon encoded within it serves as the inherited habitus that shapes the culture and individuals, but the participants in that culture reshape and modify that habitus to serve new purposes" (Staples, *The Idea of Israel*, 6–7).
[15] Staples, *The Idea of Israel*, 43–45.   [16] Staples, *The Idea of Israel*, 45.

The author of 1 Maccabees, for example, uses "'Israel' and 'Israelites' (apparently) interchangeably with 'Judaea' and *Ioudaioi*." This, Staples argues, is for a purpose, in service to Hasmonean claims to the entirety of biblical Israel: "the Hasmonean propagandist associates the Hasmonean kingdom with the more ... powerful covenantal term 'Israel.'"[17] Here we see a demonstration of the role individual intent plays in shaping interactions even with the same tradition inheritance as well as the susceptibility of the same past to multiple different identity-making discourses – multiple ways of using that past to draw boundaries between self and other. One author wanted to emphasize the importance of the Judahites within Israel, and another, to forward a political project that involved restoring Israel. So, each used the "same" story as an authoritative justification for quite different acts of boundary-making.

In addition, early, post-biblical articulations of Israelite identity also already afford us another important recognition where the overall shape of articulations of Israelite identity is concerned. In this study, again, I am writing in terms of overarching strategies and individual adaptations. But it is still important to keep in mind that even a popular, overarching strategy is only one mode of constructing the boundaries of ethnic identities, potentially among many. In this case, the true potential of ethnic expression to be articulated according to idiosyncratic, individual apprehensions is here reflected in quite an important example, the work of Philo of Alexandria, a Jewish author writing mainly in the first half of the first century CE. Philo suggested that the name Israel, etymologically speaking, meant "one who sees God," and argued as a result that Israelite identity *actually* belonged to those who deserved it most, rather than, or at least in addition to, its biological heirs.[18] In other words, it was his view that Israel would be *whichever* superior community had the capacity to *see God*, even a non-Jewish one.[19]

Yet Josephus and Philo seem to have had little influence on Jewish Late Antiquity.[20] And it does seem that, for the most part, what we can see of Jewish

---

[17] Staples, *The Idea of Israel*, 167, 170.
[18] On the likelihood that Philo was here drawing on an already extant tradition, see Harvey, *The True Israel*, 222–23.
[19] "It is an 'Israel after philosophy' rather than 'after the flesh' or 'after the spirit'" – "some of Philo's contemporary 'Jews' have this vision, but it is also available to non-Jews" (Harvey, *The True Israel*, 223). See, generally, Conf. 72, Migr. 201, Praem. 44. As Jacob Neusner observes, Philo's Israel "constitutes a philosophical category, not a social entity in the everyday sense" (Neusner, *Judaism and Its Social Metaphors*, 221). This logic, as we will see below, would appear as well in early Christian constructions of Israelite identity, including that of Justin Martyr.
[20] As the editors of a recent *Handbook of Jewish Literature from Late Antiquity* note, neither Philo nor Josephus – nor Paul – had their works "absorbed into the later tradition of Jewish thought and learning, and (as far as we know) there was no Jewish writing in Greek in the centuries with which we will be concerned, with the important exception of three separate translations of the

intellectual output in this period was most often shaped by the "biological strategy" I have described. To some extent, this is a natural development, a consequence of where the Hebrew Bible itself leaves the people Israel by the end of its story. The key text here is 2 Kings 17, the major biblical account of the Assyrian conquest of Israel which occurred at a time when the people the Bible calls Israel are actually divided between it and a kingdom called Judah. This narrative falsely claims – with considerable ramifications for the relationship between the Jewish people and Samaritan Israelites throughout history, as we will see – that the entire population of Israel was removed into Assyrian exile at that time and replaced by a variety of foreign immigrants (2 Kings 17:6, 24). Thus, from a biblical perspective, the people of Judah were already the only remaining heirs of all Israel that could be clearly identified even by the end of the eighth century BCE.[21]

What Jewish authors in the post-biblical period tended to add to this view, probably just as soon as something called Judaism can be said to exist, is simply that biblical figures were *already* Jewish. In other words, from a historian's perspective, Judaism qua Judaism – meaning the familiar touchstones of a quintessentially Jewish faith and practice – seems to have developed over the course of the last centuries BCE and the first century CE, with certain other key elements emerging even later largely as a response to the destruction of the Second Temple in 70 CE.[22] But, of course, the idea that Jewish law is on some level Mosaic law is tantamount to the idea that Moses was in many respects the archetypal Jew, and this is indeed the sensibility that emerges from early Jewish literature. In other words, for Jewish Late Antique authors, the term "Jewish" was used "in the sense that means 'linked with and continuing the Israelite

---

Hebrew Bible into Greek" (Ben-Eliyahu, Cohn, and Millar, *Handbook*, 2–3). See also Staples, *The Idea of Israel*, 254–58.

[21] As Mordecai Roshwald puts it, "[t]he term 'Jews,' strictly speaking, refers to the descendants of the tribes of Judah ... However, as the other tribes are reputed to be lost and as Jews regard themselves as continuing the historical identity of Israel as a whole, the term 'Jew' has become interchangeable with the term 'Israelite'" (Roshwald, "Marginal Jewish Sects in Israel (II)," 330).

[22] Specifically, Cohen argues that while uses of the word Ioudaios, prior to the Hasmonean rebellion of the mid second century BCE, had a largely ethnic connotation, a religious definition of the term emerges in the century following (Cohen, *The Beginnings of Jewishness*, 109). More recently, Yonatan Adler has argued that Judaism is essentially a product of those centuries "between the conquests of Alexander the Great circa 332 BCE and the founding of an independent Hasmonean polity in the middle of the second century BCE" (Adler, *The Origins of Judaism*, 20). Personally, I tend to lean toward the argument of Seth Schwartz, who notes that "the Jews were always suspended between ethnicity and religion" and that a better way of answering the question starts with asking when the distinctive practices and traditions we associate with Judaism arrived (Schwartz, "How Many Judaisms Were There?" 230).

history.'"[23] And in the Talmuds in particular, Israelite is often used to refer to people who are Jewish.[24]

One point we need to make here at the outset is that it is an open question just how prevalent the operation of the biological strategy really was where *all* the Jews of Late Antiquity are concerned. Indeed, we will see that even in the texts that I discuss further in the Element, the exclusive importance of biological descent is far more clearly in operation as a premise, and as a rhetorical claim, than as a reality. That reality, which includes multiple ways of joining and leaving the Israelite community, can, in practice, veer fairly close to the biology plus strategy described in the next section. But in addition, we need to acknowledge the great challenge of studying Israelite identity constructions in Late Antiquity, which is the challenging pattern of the evidence, extreme in character even for some corners of ancient history. This, no doubt, is part of the reason, as Catherine Hezser has recently observed, that the Jews of Late Antiquity are so often left out of discussions of Late Antiquity altogether.[25]

Basically, and especially for someone coming to this period from the study of earlier ones, there is really quite a profusion of texts, considerable in both number and variety. On the other hand, this large and varied corpus is extraordinarily *limited* in two important respects. First, while Late Antique Jews lived all over the Mediterranean and elsewhere "[a]ll the indisputably Jewish literature of these centuries which was written within the Roman Empire derives from Palestine, and the rest from Babylonia" – with a strong preponderance to the former.[26] Second, a considerably majority of it is "rabbinic" literature, which is to say it was produced by a largely insular clique of intellectual elites whose influence on other Jews of the period, especially those who lived elsewhere, is virtually unknown. Yet we know that "[m]any ancient Jews (at least until the medieval period) lived outside of rabbinic textual culture, and most diaspora populations never once set foot in Palestine or Babylonia, the places associated with rabbinic learning and textual production."[27]

---

[23] Roshwald, "Marginal Jewish Sects in Israel (II)," 330.

[24] bYevamot 69b:10 refers to "the daughter of a priest who married an Israelite," bAvodah Zarah 35b:9 to the problem of a non-Jew making milk if no "Israelite" watches him, bBerakhot 20a:5 refers to a rabbi who took a head-covering off a woman thinking she was an Israelite, bBava Metzia 24b:6 features a discussion between Rabbi Judah and Mar Shmuel about an Israelite trying to reclaim a lost purse, bYevamot 69b:1 refers to a pregnant person's "Israelite" fetus and so on and so forth. In one interesting text, bHorayot 13a:17, a quoted passage from the Mishnah offers an interesting breakdown of society – priests first, Levites second, Israelites third, then mamzers, Gibeonites, converts, and emancipated enslaved people.

[25] She notes that various recent "*Handbooks, Companions,* and *Guides* to late antiquity" even of quite recent vintage fail to devote "even one chapter to Judaism" (Hezser, "Introduction," 1).

[26] Ben-Eliyahu, Cohn, and Millar, *Handbook*, 3.

[27] Stern, *Writing on the Wall*, 10. For a survey of non-rabbinic literature, see Stemberger, "Non-Rabbinic Literature," 11–39.

As a result, we can likely guess that the average Late Antique Jew was *not* overly beholden to rabbinic constructions of who did and did not belong, let alone to rabbinic insistences about how to eat, worship, purify, and so forth. Instead, what evidence there is, which is material in nature, echoes the point I have made already: the redeployment of inherited repertoires to construct representations of self and other is by no means limited to the repertoires we might think of as belonging *specifically* to a given cultural group. Various studies, including Simcha Gross's account of the influence of Sassanid Persia on Babylonian Jewry and Karen Stern's investigation of the neglected evidence of ancient graffiti reveal perfectly clearly that Jews who lived in different parts of the Late Antique world were *of* those parts in fundamental ways.[28]

As Gross observes, for example, the evidence of "Aramaic Incantation bowls," which were created by Jewish artisans but include names with "non-Jewish theophoric elements," suggests either that Jews could have such names or that non-Jews could visit Jewish "ritual experts."[29] And as Stern clearly demonstrates, graffiti artists tended not only to write "in ways locally conventional" but to "conform to the rules of engagement in local graffiti discourse, they obey standards of content, placement, and respect for other inscriptions."[30] Evidence for cultural hybridity, rather than for sealed societies, also makes its way into cemeteries. In fact, this is the case even in the cemetery at Beth Shearim, where many of the most important Jewish leaders of the early centuries CE lie buried, including Judah "the Prince," held by tradition to be responsible for the Mishnah.[31] And in other ways too, excavations at places like Dura Europos and Nippur, the "excavated cities in Mesopotamia for which we have the strongest evidence of Jewish life," reveal how much Jewish and non-Jewish life was intertwined "in dense urban environments" – and, in Stern's words, how much the Jews of Dura in particular did not just "*interac[t]*" with "Durene society" but emerge, through their graffiti, in ways that reflect "their enmeshment in and inextricability from Durene society."[32]

---

[28] The extent to which they did so is something of a new recognition, for which, see generally Rutgers, "Archaeological Evidence," 101–18. Another study, by Rodrigo Laham Cohen, offers a survey of epigraphic evidence from all around the Mediterranean (Cohen, *The Jews in Late Antiquity*).

[29] Gross, *Babylonian Jews*, 16–17. Shana Strauch Schick and Steven Fine observe that "the mosaic floor of the Samarian synagogue at Beit Shean was laid by the same craftsmen who also created the mosaic of the Beit Alpha synagogue" belonging to the Jews (Schick and Fine, "Do You Have an Onion?" 73).

[30] Stern, *Writing on the Wall*, 65.

[31] Even here, Stern argues that "works of Jewish commemorators and inscribers reflect understandings about death, corpse contagion, and commemorative practice with closer ties to regional non-Jewish behavior than to rabbinic textual prescription" (Stern, *Writing on the Wall*, 83).

[32] Gross, *Babylonian Jews*, 19; Stern, *Writing on the Wall*, 57.

Yet we are, unfortunately, much more able to be specific about how the boundaries of ethnic identity are constructed from literary evidence than from material. And this brings us back to the Talmuds – and the Babylonian in particular – because they also happen to deal with questions of identity in great detail. Here we encounter quite a clear series of representations of the thesis I am pursuing, that ethnicities are indeed not defined by a stable set of contents handed down through the generations. If they were, we would expect there to be a consensus between those who articulate visions of the ethnic group through appeals to tradition inheritances, as to what these inheritances *mean*. Instead, what we see is that two different authors can put quite different casts on the same story or have quite different ideas about *which* the authorizing inheritances should be.

Here it might be useful to pause for just a moment to introduce the corpus of rabbinic literature, as it is understood in both tradition and reality.[33] In tradition, as Max K. Strassfeld has recently observed, the basic idea is that much of early rabbinic literature was an attempt to put back together what the destruction of Jerusalem had broken apart.[34] The internal chronology of rabbinic composition, and in certain respects, the scholarly chronology, is organized according to a series of rabbinic eras, further subdivided into discrete rabbinic generations. In tradition, the first era, that of the Tannaim or "teachers," is linked to the world of the Second Temple through the person of Yohanan ben Zakkai, who was smuggled out of burning Jerusalem in a coffin. From there, he would found the rabbinic academy at Yavneh that enabled post-Temple Judaism to put down strong roots.[35] To the Tannaim, supposedly, belong the Mishnah, traditionally attributed to Judah the Prince, or Judah ha-Nasi, around the turn of the third century CE, as well as many other tremendously influential texts.[36]

---

[33] There is also early Jewish literature that is not rabbinic, for which, see Stemberger, "Non-Rabbinic Literature."

[34] Strassfeld, *Trans Talmud*, 10.

[35] As Strack and Stemberger observe, this is made literal in certain texts. "There is a break after Hillel and Shammai: after them, only Yohanan ben Zakkai is described in the same language of tradition (*qibbel- masar*), while the appended list of patriarchs and the enumeration of the other rabbis does not employ this typical terminology. This illustrates the desire to link Yohanan with the 'pairs', i.e. to connect the rabbinic with the Pharisaic tradition" (Strack and Stemberger, *Introduction*, 4).

[36] These include the Tosefta, an additional collection of mostly halakhic teachings, and various rabbinic commentaries known as the Midrash Halakhah: The Mekhilta of Rabbi Ishmael, the Sifra on Leviticus, a commentary on Leviticus, the Sifre, on Numbers, an identically titled commentary on Deuteronomy, and a few other odds and ends. I am grateful to Daniel Picus for his advice on how to frame this complicated reality in a gloss. In tradition, Judah was working off of an already extant core that had been produced through the oral teachings of Rabbi Akiva and the intermediary work of his student Rabbi Meir. One still probably-too-credible but influential vision of the role of Akiva and Meir appears in Strack and Stemberger, who argue that "[a]s for R. Aqiba, whom according to Sanh 86a all follow, his importance for the development of the

Israel and Its Heirs in Late Antiquity 11

Next, in the traditional picture, came the Amoraim, or "speakers," who were active until roughly the end of the fifth century CE. Where the production of the Talmuds is concerned these are supposed to have produced the Palestinian and Babylonian Gemara, commentaries on the Mishnah that are distinguished from each other by who contributed to them, when they were finished, and, indeed, which "tractates" of the Mishnah they comment on. Both sets of Gemara include references to Palestinian and Babylonian rabbis. However, the Palestinian Talmud, which was supposed to have been finished in the early fifth century, includes various tractates of the Mishnah and the Gemara produced in Palestine, while the Babylonian Talmud is supposed – by the Talmud itself! – to have been finished in the days of Rabbis Ashi and Ravina, both Babylonian Rabbis, in the late fifth century.[37] In other words, the Palestinian combination of Mishnah and Gemara formed the Palestinian Talmud, the Babylonian combination the Babylonian – with, even in the traditional view, some editing left to the "Saboraim" or "reasoners," active until around 600 CE.

As I will discuss in the conclusion, much of this timeline now seems inaccurate, traditional attributions seem both harder to prove and harder to accept, and even this rendition of tradition fails to reflect just how strongly traditional views emphasize the continuity between talmudic literature and a Jewish history stretching back to Moses. In other words, we certainly do now believe that the Talmuds were in production for longer, considered open for longer, and more dramatically shaped by later authors and editors than prior generations of scholars suggested. But it is partially for that reason that I focus particularly on the Babylonian Talmud here, since it is an object example, in miniature, of the problems inherent in modeling the nature of the relationship between traditions and their heirs in terms of continuity rather than dynamic reinvention. This topic, too, I will return to in the conclusion.

For now, however, consider the example of the story of the man from Nehardea, as related in bKiddushin 70a-b. The story begins when Rabbi

---

M [Mishnah] tradition is undoubted . . . Our question here, however, is not the extent of Aqiba's contribution to the *material* of M, but whether Aqiba created an ordered, edited M collection which is still identifiable by *literary criteria*" (Strack and Stemberger, *Introduction*, 131). Ultimately, they conclude that "[i]f Aqiba did create a proto-Mishnah, this must have been completely absorbed in the work of his students" (Strack and Stemberger, *Introduction*, 132).

[37] Strack and Stemberger, *Introduction*, 212–13. There is some confusion as to precisely when this would have been because there were two Ravinas who lived in the fifth century CE. Ravina I died in the early fifth century CE, and Ravina II probably around 500. This view of the role of Ashi and Ravina rests on two references in the Talmud, bBaba Batra 157b, which refers to the "edition" or "revision" of Ashi and bBaba Metzia 86a which "calls Rabbi and R. Nathan the end of the *Mishnah,* Rab Ashi and Rabina the end of the *hor'ah,*" a complicated word that has something to do with "a particular form of the teaching and authoritative decision of the halakhah" (Strack and Stemberger, *Introduction*, 192).

Judah bar Ezekiel, best known for founding the important rabbinic academy at Pumbedita, sends a servant of his to buy meat at the butcher shop. Once there, a rude man cuts in line in front of him and, when rebuked, insults the rabbi himself. In the end, this minor incident sets a series of events in motion that would not end until it had carved a wide swathe of social devastation through all of Nehardea – and until Judah himself was almost stoned to death by the outraged citizenry.

In a nutshell: the rabbi first excommunicated the man from Nehardea, which, he says, is the punishment for insulting a sage, but then goes well beyond this judgment to rule that the man's very lineage was suspect. As a result, he was no longer entitled to marry someone of pure Jewish lineage (70a). When the man showed up in person to complain, claiming that he was a descendant of no lesser lineage than that of the Hasmonean (Maccabean) kings themselves, Rabbi Judah responds by referring to a tradition in which the only survivors of the Hasmoneans were the enslaved of that house (70b), thus justifying his already pronounced judgment. As a result of this proclamation apparently quite a few marriages were annulled and "several marriage contracts were torn up" (70b).[38] This, naturally, is when a mob arrived to stone the rabbi, but he saved himself by threatening to reveal still more unpure lineages unless they let him go.

On the one hand, we can obviously say about this incident that it offers a clear reflection of the biological strategy in action and of the extreme consequences of finding oneself on the outs. Israelite identity is determined by descent, the rabbi finds the man lacks it, and as a result he, and many families along with him, no longer belong. The social fabric of their lives is torn apart; they are outcasts, and certainly unfit for Jewish marriage. At the same time, consider how Rabbi Judah actually applies the biological strategy here. How, after all, does he determine that the man from Nehardea lacks the pedigree to be considered a full member of the Jewish community? He does not study any genealogical records; he is not relying on any previously secret knowledge about the man's background vouchsafed to him. Instead, once Judah learns that the man had a tendency to insult others by referring to them as enslaved (70b), he argues that this by itself is the proof that the man's own lineage is flawed, and specifically by descent from the enslaved. As justification, he cites a saying of his own teacher, Rabbi Samuel of Nehardea: "he disqualifies with his own flaw" (70b).

Obviously, Rabbi Judah is citing an inherited, authoritative quotation to make a judgment about the borders of Israelite identity. But it is not as if every other authority would use this particular quotation in the same way, or even interpret it

---

[38] Talmudic translations from Sefaria.org unless otherwise noted, and specifically the William Davidson edition of the Babylonian Talmud.

as Judah does. In fact, in the story itself, Rabbi Nahman, judge of Nehardea, demurs when confronted with Judah's explanation of Samuel's words.[39] He wonders, reasonably, whether such a statement as Samuel's can be taken so seriously as to constitute an *entirely* sufficient case against a litigant (70b). The revelation of the man's Hasmonean claims, which come in the story *after* Nahman's rebuttal and allow Judah to add to his judgment an argument based on a tradition he knew about the Hasmonean royal house, is presumably intended to vindicate Judah – and this extremely fraught way of doing boundary-making business with him. But it is perfectly clear, up to that moment, that someone else would draw the boundaries of society in a different way, even with the same authorizing traditions in hand.

This same dynamic is clearly at play in much of the rest of bKiddushin 70b-71a, which, if it is about any one thing, is indeed about how complex the task of applying inherited traditions to practical matters of contemporary ethnic construction is. At one point, Rabbi Judah makes further pronouncements, claiming that the people of Gova'ai and Dorenunita are Gibeonites, a people mentioned in the Bible who joined the Israelite community in the days of Joshua by subterfuge. Obviously, even knowing that there are Gibeonites out there, two different authors might not only decide that they are represented by different groups but treat the significance of this discovery differently, arguing that Gibeonites, who entered Israel so long ago, deserve to be entirely included.

Next, Judah tells the story of a biblical figure, Pashur ben Immer, a priest who is mentioned in the book of Jeremiah. According to Judah, Pashur was such an impressive figure that four hundred or even four thousand of his enslaved people came to be regarded as priests themselves – which means that any number of contemporaneous priestly descendants may also have flawed lineages, like the man of Nehardea. Once again, Judah applies quite a subjective test, taken from Rabbi Samuel: if a priest is insolent, they are the descendant of an enslaved person, because insolence is a quality revealing descent from Pashur's priests (70b). Once again, another rabbi suggests that the issue is not so cut and dry. Rabbi Elazar notes a biblical text, Hosea 4:4, which implies that priests can be argumentative – even with unflawed descent – and suggests that the better part of wisdom is refusing to speculate on the basis of such limited evidence.

Finally, the text considers the problem of what will happen to families of uncertain descent in times to come. Rabbi Avin bar Rav, in the name of Rav, says that those with flawed lineage can never truly become a member of the tribes of Israel at all, which is to say, there is a sense in which they are not really

---

[39] Simcha Gross correctly notes that this and other similar stories in the Talmuds certainly reflect the competition between "Jewish elites" over status and hierarchy (Gross, *Babylonian Jews*, 86–87).

Israelites. Hama bar Hanina agrees, at least, that the divine presence rests only upon those of unflawed lineage (70b). But, other rabbis, including Hama bar Hanina himself and Joshua ben Levi discuss circumstances in which lineages may indeed be purified, by God, or, in fact, by wealth, in the sense that a wealthy "mamzer" – someone conceived illegitimately – can find a marriage partner regardless of their impurity (71a). Rabbi Isaac concludes, in a comment on these transformations, and contra some of the authorities just mentioned, that "a family that has become assimilated with Jews of unflawed lineage remains assimilated" and "are not removed from their tribes despite their flawed lineage," even at the end of time. Other discussions in the same section of the Talmud concern whether one should presume that Jewish families in different places have flawed or unflawed lineages, and there are a variety of reflections on the danger of commenting on potential flaws in the lineage of powerful families in particular. There is one suggestion that Elijah himself must ultimately determine which lineages are flawed and unflawed. In this last case, the text seems of two minds: Abaye holds that if a family has become assimilated, but no one knows it, Elijah will not make it known either – in which case, presumably, families of flawed lineage will be treated like any other.[40] And of course even these aspirationally exhaustive treatments leave certain stones unturned. What happens if someone's ancestor was a Gibeonite, or an enslaved priest, but the lineage was later purified – and then their descendant is either insulting or insolent?

Where the overall argument of this section is concerned, of course, the most important point is that each of these passages, in its own way, shows how reductive it is to simply identify an overarching strategy, and to characterize that strategy as tantamount to what ethnic identity *is*, as opposed to thinking of ethnicity as how that strategy, or other strategies, are applied in particular contexts. In other words, if we just said, "in the Talmuds, Israelite identity is understood as a matter of biological descent," we would, in fact, have no way of knowing who was actually understood to belong to the ethnos in Rabbi Judah's purview, as opposed to Rabbi Nahman's or Rabbi Elazar's, because they have different ideas on this score. Only an active understanding – only the idea that ethnicity is what it does – can actually account for the range of identity phenomenon we encounter in surviving texts. As a result, there is indeed no

---

[40] Chance McMahon-Harrer has drawn my attention to M.Yadayim 4:4, as well, in which an Ammonite convert asks to enter the house of study, is forbidden by Rabbi Gamaliel on the basis of Deut 23:4's admonition against allowing Ammonites and Moabites into the assembly, but is invited by Rabbi Joshua on the basis of Isaiah 10:1, which speaks of "removing the bounds of the peoples." Not only that, Joshua argues that the Assyrian conquest so mingled all the peoples that old distinctions can no longer hold.

"real" biological Israel that exists apart from how Israelite identity is defined by those in a position to define it, like the various rabbinic sages. There is only how ethnic discourses are actually used in a given context. This is the dynamic tension between fixity and fluidity that Buell has argued ethnicity is, and this is a reflection of the fluidity a fixed starting point is capable of achieving when deployed in actual acts of identifying. Then, different people will have different views on who might be a Gibeonite, or a mamzer, or different understandings of what is possible for the family of someone who becomes affiliated with the Israelite people for some reason or another.

Another way to put it is that "Gibeonite," "Hasmonean," and "Pashur" are terms in the repertoire for articulating what is shared and not shared that comes from the past. But authors can always tell new stories and offer new interpretations that take the apparent meaning of these terms in a new direction. They can always "discover" that someone, or some place, is, or is not, within the compass of the people Israel – according to a supposedly age-old tradition, or inherited wisdom, newly "understood." And in addition, what we receive from the past is a far less constrained category than it seemed to be in a Romantic model of a tradition inheritance handed down through the generations. Again, in my previous study, I explored this conclusion with respect to "becoming Israel," which is to say, the fact that a group might suddenly "decide" that their ancestors were Israelites, rather than somebody else, gestured at the fact that we are not required to build the next generation of identity constructions only out of the set of traditions from which they were built by our ancestors.

In the Talmuds, because there are so many different potential sources of rabbinic wisdom and judgment, the same dynamic is operational. In fact, we can consider the "baraitot," the plural of "baraita," Aramaic for "external," which are rabbinic quotations commented upon in the Talmuds that come from somewhere besides the Mishnah. While some of these come from other authoritative early collections, such as the Tosefta, others have no known source at all.[41] If we imagine rabbis engaged in the business of drawing on received wisdom, but suppose that the pool of received wisdom is much larger than we are used to thinking, *and* that they can do more different things with it than we might expect, then we will get a truer sense of how inventive efforts to construct an ethnic identity can be.

In addition, it is of course the case that even someone who wishes only to translate the plain meaning of an inherited tradition to posterity may not

---

[41] "Baraitot in the two Talmuds do not have parallels in the tannaitic collection ... it is unclear whether they were invented in post-tannaitic times, perhaps even Babylonia, or whether they are authentic tannaitic teachings external to both the Mishnah and the Tosefta" (Kulp and Rogoff, *Reconstructing the Talmud*, 23).

understand what that plain meaning *is* in the same way as someone else.[42] Indeed, we might think of an observation Moulie Vidas makes about the Geonim, heads of the great Jewish academies who were the generational heirs of those whose efforts produced the main body of the Talmuds: that they often attributed "to an Amoraic sage a statement that the stam offers in that sage's defense."[43] The "stam," as I will discuss in greater detail elsewhere in this Element, is the final, anonymous editorial layer of the text. But what this means is that we have an example here where even those invested with the most traditional authority, and considered, by their constituents, to be the most skilled at reading and interpreting the relevant texts understand something as basic as who says what differently from other experts. These kinds of differences in basic apprehension show why it is impossible for so many different authors to simply pass down inherited traditions in precisely the same way, even if they intend to do just that.

When we turn to the bigger picture with these lessons in mind, I think both the operation of the biological strategy in the hands of different authors and the fluidity of ethnic discourse more generally is especially visible in two contexts, within the Talmuds and in early Jewish literature more generally. The first is a context in which we might expect the biological strategy to render one outcome, but the other appears to be more common: rabbinic discussions of converts and their role in the Israelite community. The second is one in which the same boundary is consistently drawn, but in a wide variety of different ways, with wildly different justifications oriented toward the "past": the exclusion of the Samaritan Israelites from the Jewish community.

In the first case, there certainly were those who held that converts, who by definition are not biological descendants of the original Israelites, could never be fully included in the community. Rabbi Chelbo, for example, describes converts as "scabs" on the body of the Jewish people (bKid. 70b, bYev. 47b, bNidd. 13b). And in bNiddah 13b a saying is attributed to "the Sages" in a "baraita" – again, a quote from something that is not in the Mishnah – in which converts are among those who "delay the coming of the Messiah." On the other hand, as Shaye Cohen has observed, not only do many other texts come to different conclusions, they often do so with what he identifies as an implicit sense of surprise. In other words, he suggests the presence of a "standard rhetorical pattern ... 'I might have thought that 'Israel' excluded converts, but Scripture adds some other phrase to imply their inclusion.'"[44] As examples, Cohen points to the tension between texts like Mishnah Bikkurim 1:4–5, which

---

[42] See the discussion in Tobolowsky, "The Thor Movies," 173–86.
[43] Vidas, *Tradition and the Formation of the Talmud*, 210.
[44] Cohen, *The Beginnings of Jewishness*, 337–38.

insists that "[t]he people 'Israel' are linked to each other by common descent from a single set of 'fathers.' The category 'Israel' as a concrete social reality, is first and foremost a function of pedigree, genealogy, and birth" and the lived reality, from other texts, that "the rabbis did permit gentiles to enter: converts could take their place within the community of Israel, become Jews, and marry Israelites of good standing."[45] As what he refers to as the rabbinic conversion ceremony declares – from bYevamot47a-b, reiterated in the post-Talmudic tractate Gerim – the convert "is like an Israelite in all respects."[46]

In addition, Cohen emphasizes the presence of Talmudic texts which simply do not seem to share the strict sense of the boundaries of Israel that is visible elsewhere. He points to the Gemara in the Jerusalem Talmud which follows on the aforementioned Mishnaic verse from Bikkurim, in which Rabbi Judah argues that all converts have an Israelite father in Abraham (pBikk 1:4 64a). Here, Judah is referring to Genesis 17:4–5, when God declares Abraham the ancestor of many nations.[47] Obviously, the fact that this text exists in an authoritative collection, even in the most important authoritative collection, the Bible itself, means that the argument that *biological* Israel could be bigger than the family of Jacob also exists in potentia at all times. The fact that somebody in the Jerusalem Talmud used it in just that way shows how potential can become reality even when it seems surprising from the outside that it should.[48] Indeed, even in bKiddushin 70b itself, with its challenges to established Jewish families and priests, Rabbah bar Rav Huna seems to say that a convert *can* become fully part of the people Israel – quoting Jeremiah 30:21–22, "you shall be my people, and I will be your God" – when they draw themselves near to God (70b). Again, Rabbi Isaac, in 71a, states that "a family that has become assimilated with Jews of unflawed lineage remains assimilated" (71a). In bYevamot 47b a convert is investigated as to whether he is really committed to following all the mitzvot, and if so, it is considered a mitzvah to convert him.[49]

---

[45] Cohen, *The Beginnings of Jewishness*, 337. See, for example, M. Bikk 1:4, which says that a convert cannot refer to "our fathers" as in Deut 26:3 but should say "the God of your fathers" unless his mother was an Israelite, in which case he can say it. For the conversion ceremony, see Cohen, *The Beginnings of Jewishness*, 199–202.

[46] Cohen, *The Beginnings of Jewishness*, 336–37. He notes as well the great uncertainty where the date of Tractate Gerim is concerned, "first attested explicitly about 1300," which is why no longer discussion of it appears here (Cohen, *The Beginnings of Jewishness*, 211).

[47] Cohen, *The Beginnings of Jewishness*, 328–30.

[48] This, it is worth acknowledging, echoes another discourse, in Tractate Gerim, which notes that Abraham was in fact a convert, and referred to himself as a "ger," foreigner (Ger. 4.3). For an insightful discussion of how fluid biblical traditions could be in the hands of the rabbis, see Wollenberg, *The Closed Book*.

[49] Moshe Lavee describes bYevamot 46–48 as a "mini-tractate" on conversion, in which Amoraic rabbis attributed their views and norms to Tannaitic authorities (Lavee, "The 'Tractate' of Conversion," 169–213).

Thus, Lawrence Schiffman, too, has argued that "converts and freed slaves were considered full-fledged Jews by Tannaitic halakhah."[50] Louis Feldman has chronicled quite a few authorities who have positive things to say on this subject: Rabbis Yohanan and Eleazar in bPesahim 86b, Johanan in bNedarim 32a, Abbahu in Tanhuma Genesis Vayetze 22, and Leviticus Rabbah 11.2. Feldman notes that in the Jerusalem Talmud, Abbahu says in the name of Yohanan that the daughter of a mixed marriage can marry even the high priest and say a first fruits prayer that belongs to the Israelites (yYevamot 8:3 9 c, yBikkurim 1:4 64a).[51] These honors, of course, are generally reserved for full members of the Israelite community, so the rabbi's implication here is clear: the child of a convert is a biological Israelite for all intents and purposes.

On the one hand, then, the biological strategy clearly could be taken so seriously, at least in literature, that someone's insults or arrogance in even one instance could jeopardize their claim to being an Israelite altogether by apparently revealing tainted lineage. On the other, there were many who believed that even those whose ancestors were not Israelites could more or less fully become biological Israelites. For those who wished to pursue either path, the profusion of genealogical data in the Hebrew Bible itself provided ready options, and a wide variety of other texts and oral teachings did as well. Indeed, it is worth saying that an argument that descent from Abraham made someone a potential member of the Israelite community is a biological strategy, too, calibrated differently.

In addition, as with the example of Philo, it is of course the case that other strategies besides the biological strategy could be deployed in various texts, either on their own or in conjunction. While there is not much room to discuss it here, we can say briefly that these include texts where the determining factor for Israelite identity can seem to be ritual practice, rather than descent – or rather, as an additional element, between those who shared descent – which is to say, more or less what we see in the next set of "biology plus" examples discussed in the relevant places. In bAvodah Zarah 76b, for example, Mar Yehuda and Bati Bar Tuvi have an audience with Shapur, king of Persia. Shapur offers a slice of etrog to Bati bar Tuvi, then eats one himself, *then* purifies the knife before offering a slice to Mar Yehuda. Bati objects that he should get the same treatment as Mar Yehuda, being a fellow Jew, but Shapur responds that he is unsure of Bati's Jewishness because he is not "meticulous about *halakha*." As Gross observes, it is explicitly "the Jewish identity of Mar Yehuda" that the king questions, based not on descent but practice.[52]

---

[50] Schiffman, "The Samaritans in Tannaitic Halakhah," 329.
[51] Feldman, "Proselytism," 408–409. [52] Gross, *Babylonian Jews*, 248.

In other cases, even geography could be used as a dividing line. In bKetubot 110b, the teaching is related that it is better for someone to reside in Palestine, even among mostly gentile neighbors, than anywhere else even with mostly Jewish neighbors and further states that "anyone who resides outside of Eretz Israel" is regarded "as though he is engaged in idol worship." In the Tosefta, Avodah Zarah 5 makes the same point. Each of these suggests that features external to questions of descent could be used as an arbiter of descent, if necessary. We might even say it shows that even those who understood themselves to be proponents of a biological understanding of ethnicity could find themselves in situations where their own understandings shifted to respond to complex realities, like the problem of converts or the need to define themselves further against co-ethnics who had suspect practices.[53]

As for the Samaritan Israelites, what talmudic responses to their inclusion most help reveal – prior to the extensive discussion of this group in the following section – is just how incredibly flexible ethnic boundary-making discourse could be and how many different ways individual authors could decide to make their cases. On the one hand, there is an overarching or at least common strategy in the Talmuds for dealing with the difference between Samaritan Israelite and Jewish identity that is an iteration of the biological strategy. It is based on 2 Kings 17, and really in two respects. First, this text claims that the Samaritan Israelites are the descendants of one of the groups brought in by the Assyrians, the "Kutheans," which is what they are usually called in the Talmuds. Second, there is a story in 2 Kings 17:25–28 in which these foreigners only converted to Yahwism because they were attacked by vicious lions. Thus, in the Talmuds, Rabbi Ishmael disqualifies them by referring to them as "lion converts" though a tradition is also mentioned in which Rabbi Akiva refutes this view (bQid. 75a-b, yGit. 1:5 43 c).[54] Other texts feature a lively debate about whether a Samaritan Israelite is "like an Israelite" – an opinion attributed to Simeon ben Gamaliel in the Tosefta – or "like a Gentile," as his interlocutor Judah ha-Nasi holds (tTer. 4:12; 4:14). What is meant by these statements depends on who you ask, but the text certainly shows how different authorities could look at the same inherited traditions and come to different conclusions about what they meant for boundary construction.

In the Talmuds themselves, however, what we really see in this case is how much the desire to draw a boundary can shape how inherited materials are actually used. This is particularly visible in a passage from the Jerusalem Talmud. Here, in yGittin, the question is introduced, "Why is the Samaritan

---

[53] I am grateful to Andrew Jacobs for this suggestion.
[54] Schiffman, "The Samaritans in Tannaitic Halakhah," 327.

disqualified?," to which Rabbi Yohanan gives the familiar answer that they are lion converts (yGit. 1:5 43c). This time, however, the questioner acknowledges that their *ancestors* were lion converts but points out that if "true converts" are to be accepted into the community, then there is no reason that the descendants of these lion converts cannot now be true converts. Now, however, the argument shifts – the issue is that Samaritan Israelite exclusion is actually due to marriage impurity. They are not Jews, and so their children are mamzers. The questioner returns again to point out that Akiva (is supposed to have) said that they were genuine converts, and is now told they are excluded because they do not practice levirate marriage, then that they do not perform divorces properly – Gamaliel says they do – and finally that the real issue is that their lineage is intermingled with "priests of the High Places," which is to say, priests whom the Bible regards as performing improper worship.

Other texts reflect a similarly fluid approach to the problem of Samaritan Israelite difference, including Avodah Zarah in the Palestinian Talmud. Here, Rabbi Abbahu offers many different explanations for why Samaritan wine is forbidden (yAz 5:4 44d): that they secretly buy wine from Gentiles, that Diocletian forced the Samaritan Israelites, but not the Jews, to offer libations with their wine, or even that the Samaritan Israelites had some kind of idol – a dove – that they offer libations to, making their wine impure.[55] He also offers the view, when asked by the Samaritan Israelites in person, that they had *become* too impure to share wine with the Jews only recently, but that they are now so impure as to be considered essentially gentiles – one cannot even eat their parboiled food. In short, in both cases, the conclusion is the same – the Samaritan Israelite is not to be included – but the person reaching it visibly tries different tactics to maintain it against challenges, whatever is needed to refute the argument for inclusion that is being made at that time.

Then, turning to the wider world of early Jewish articulations of Israelite identity, we see something really remarkable: that even the idea that 2 Kings 17 explains the reasons for Samaritan Israelite exclusion fails to incapsulate the full range of boundary-making phenomenon where this group is concerned. Some texts, cutting quite against the biological strategy, even forthrightly acknowledge their (biological) Israelite descent, but still disqualify them on other grounds with reference to other stories. So, for example, Matthew Chalmers observes that in 4 Baruch, an apocryphal work concerning the Babylonian conquest of Jerusalem from the first or second century CE, the Samaritans are

---

[55] See the discussion in Schick and Fine, "Do You Have an Onion?" 73–74. Angel observes that in the Chronicle of Abu l-Fath, the Samaritans level a parallel accusation: "How the emperor Hadrian ... upon entering the Holy of Holies of the Jerusalem temple, observed the statue that the Jews had been worshipping" (Angel, "'Kinsmen' or an 'Alien Race?'" 54).

actually understood not just as Israelites but *Judahites*.[56] In this case, however, they were evicted from the community because their ancestors refused to give up their foreign wives when Ezra and Nehemiah demand it of them.

As a result, they are barred from Jerusalem by Jeremiah, his scribe, the eponymous Baruch, and the faithful Ethiopian Abimelech (8:6–8).[57] After attempting to return to Babylon, where they are also turned away, they then establish the city of Samaria (8:11–12), and, of course, finally become Samaritan Israelites. In addition, Chalmers mentions the "Ascension of Isaiah," in which a Samaritan protagonist named Belchira, the descendant of false – but Israelite – prophets flees to Judah during the Assyrian conquest and conspires to have Isaiah executed.[58] In other words, this is a text that acknowledges the legitimacy of the Israelite lineage of the Samaritan Israelites but delegitimizes them on the basis of their ancestors' bad behavior. And there may even have been some – probably not the rabbis, but certain Christian authors at any rate – who felt that the Samaritans descended not from Kutheans but from the Canaanites.[59]

Thus, we see repeatedly that authors who articulate constructions of ethnic identity return to a shared set of authoritative texts, but there is no one set thing to do with them, and the boundaries of the shared set is itself not absolute. The starting point for many acts of boundary-making was indeed the main strategy I have been interested in: the "biological" strategy, the idea that the Jewish people are the only true heirs of Israel because they are the only true biological descendants of the biblical people. Yet even here there was a wide array of ways to understand how to actually apply this view when in the business of making borders as a practical matter, and even a relatively widespread recognition that converts could become something much like biological Israelites by adoption. Also even here, where it is so prevalent, it is still clear enough that the biological strategy was just one strategy among many for policing boundaries, which included ways to establish who really belonged and who didn't even among

---

[56] Chalmers, "Viewing Samaritans Jewishly," 351–52. Here he refers to the longer version, from Greek witnesses.
[57] Chalmers, "Viewing Samaritans Jewishly," 352. See Charlesworth, *Old Testament Pseudepigrapha*, 423–24.
[58] Chalmers, "Viewing Samaritans Jewishly," 350.
[59] As Schiffman observes, some, like Gedaliah Alon, have made the case that this idea appears in the Tannaitic period as well, but Schiffman believes it is only visible in Amoraic texts, and perhaps not even there (Schiffman, "The Samaritans in Tannaitic Halakhah," 325; Alon, "The Origin of the Samaritans in the Halakhic Tradition," 354–73). It does, however, appear in some "Greco-Roman sources" (325). This, presumably, includes the *Panarion* of Epiphanius of Salamis from the late fourth century CE, where, among quite a number of descriptions of these people, the Salamnian bishop derives the name Samaritan from one Somoron, son of Somer, "one of the Perizzites and Girgashites who inhabited the land at that time" (Pan 9.1). See the translation in Epiphanius and Williams, *The Panarion of Epiphanius of Salamis*, 32.

biological descendants, as in the story of King Shapur and Mar Yehuda. And there was always, always, the potential for a new approach altogether, one likely to be drawn from a shared repertoire of inherited stories, but given new prominence, or seen in a new light.

Samaritan Israelite Constructions of Israelite Identity in Late Antiquity

The history of the Samaritan Israelites presents a problem from which – to paraphrase James Joyce – a certain amount of scholarship is still trying to awaken. Until quite recently, that history was usually narrated, outside of the community, through the lens of 2 Kings 17, which appeared to make the Samaritan Israelites the descendants of foreign immigrants. In recent years, scholarship has come to acknowledge what the Samaritan Israelites have always claimed: that they are, for the most part, the descendants of the Israelites of Israel rather than Judah.[60] But, this does not precisely vindicate Samaritan Israelite tradition *itself* in the eyes of the historian, any more than the fact of Jewish descent mainly from the Israelites of Judah vindicates the tradition that makes Moses into an archetypal Jew.

Indeed, the histories of the Jews and Samaritan Israelites are usefully parallel. Much as in the Jewish case, a distinctly Samaritan Israelite identity seems to have emerged between the last centuries BCE and the first century CE, in some ways in continuity with earlier articulations of Israelite identity and practice and in some ways discontinuous with them.[61] Broadly speaking, Samaritan Israelite identity seems to have developed around three touchstones: a particular devotion to Mt. Gerizim, the Samaritan Israelite Pentateuch, and what Stefan Schorch has called "an exclusive tradition, implying that their authenticity as 'Israel' is true in both historical and religious terms."[62] The middle piece of this puzzle, which emerged out of the same milieu as the biblical Pentateuch, especially points to the importance of the late centuries BCE in the formation of Samaritan Israelite identity.[63] Then, over the course of the first centuries CE, Samaritan Israeliteism, like Judaism, took on ever more of its familiar shape –

---

[60] See, especially, Knoppers, *Jews and Samaritans*.
[61] There are some outlier arguments – Etienne Nodet's that the early Israelites were indeed already Samaritan Israelites, and Magnar Kartveit's that Samaritan Israelite identity emerged with the construction of the temple on Mt. Gerizim in the fifth century BCE. See Nodet, *The Samaritans*; Kartveit, *The Origins of the Samaritans*.
[62] Schorch, "The Construction of Samari(t)an Identity," 135.
[63] Tobolowsky, *The Myth of the Twelve Tribes of Israel*, 66–79. See also Stefan Schorch, "A Critical Editio Maior," 1–21; Adrian Schenker, "Le Seigneur Choisira-t-Il Le Lieu de Son Nom Ou l'a-t-Il Choisi?" 339–51; Eshel and Eshel, "Dating the Samaritan Pentateuch's Compilation."

according to tradition, especially through the intercession of the Samaritan Israelite holy man, Baba Rabba.[64]

Unfortunately for the particular goals of this study, it is really very difficult to say almost anything about Samaritan Israelite constructions of Israelite identity in Late Antiquity itself with any certainty because of an absence of surviving stories from this period. This is not to say that there are no Samaritan Israelite *texts* from Late Antiquity, some of which I will discuss later on. Indeed, we may have some brief excerpts that go back as far as the Hellenistic period, surviving in Eusebius' *Praeperatio Evangelica*, for example. These include fragments of a supposedly second-century BCE epic poem by one Theodotus.[65] But, for the period in question, the surviving material is not historiographical but interpretive and liturgical: chiefly, the Samaritan targum, which is to say, an Aramaic version of the Samaritan Pentateuch, and a relatively large body of liturgical poetry.[66] These are rich with Samaritan Israelite ideology but do not contain explicit descriptions of what makes a Samaritan Israelite different from *other* groups, which leaves us needing to fill in the gaps.

In addition, an underappreciated problem stems from a well-known fact about the Samaritan Israelites – that is, they have *only* a canonical Pentateuch. In other words, where Jewish understandings of scripture encompass books that relate explicitly to the eras when different parts of Israel went their separate ways – the books of Kings, Chronicles, Ezra, and Nehemiah in particular – the canonical account of Samaritan Israelite identity ends with the death of Moses. The Samaritan Pentateuch does reflect what was already, or would become, Samaritan Israelite difference in some ways, including references to an altar Moses set up on Gerizim (Deut 27:4) and a reference to Gerizim in the Samaritan Israelite version of the ten commandments in Exodus (20:17), both of which are missing from the biblical text.[67] But it does not tell us how early Samaritan Israelites understood how they came to be different from other Israelites in historical terms the way the Hebrew Bible does because it offers no parallel account of these eras.

Meanwhile, there *are* Samaritan Israelite traditions about these and other important developments in Samaritan Israelite history but they are from too *late*

---

[64] Pummer, *The Samaritans*, 132–33.

[65] These, however, are not in Samaritan manuscripts, and it is often difficult to feel confident about their true origins (Pummer, *The Samaritans*, 219–20). See also Crown, "Samaritan Literature," 24–25. John Collins has argued that Theodotus was not a Samaritan, for which see Collins, "The Epic of Theodotus," 91–104.

[66] See the discussion in Pummer, *The Samaritans*, 208–11, 239–41.

[67] "... the MT and the SP are close to one another in many respects. This fact is obscured in many modern treatments of the SP, which speak of some 6,000 textual variations between them ... But the 6,000 figure is quite misleading, because most of the variants are rather minor in nature" (Knoppers, *Jews and Samaritans*, 179). See also Fine, "The Consolation of Souls," 21–25.

a period. In other words, there are any number of stories in what are usually called the Samaritan Israelite "chronicles" but these range in date from the medieval period all the way up to the twentieth century, at least in terms of when they were actually finished.[68] The most important are the *Asatir*, which may date from the tenth century; the *Tulidah*, from the mid-twelfth; the *Kitab al-Tarikh of Abu l'Fath*, in the mid-fourteenth; the "Samaritan book of Joshua," a compilation published "by an unnamed Samaritan scholar in the thirteenth century;" the "New Chronicle," "Chronicle Adler," or "Sefer Hayamim," which is supposed to continue the book of Joshua to the late nineteenth century; and the "Chronicle II." The last two date to the late nineteenth or the turn of the twentieth century, in their present form.[69]

The result, such as it is, is that the scholar who is interested in reconstructing *Late Antique* constructions of Israelite identity must do one of two things, and preferably both. They can attempt to read into what little survives from Late Antiquity, and they can make assumptions about what these much later collections can tell us about earlier eras. What I will argue is that both, in their way, reveal the operation of what I have called the "biology plus" strategy in Samaritan Israelite efforts to distinguish themselves from the Jewish people as Israelites. In my view, this consisted of an understanding that the Samaritan Israelites were *not* the only biological Israelites around – but that, nevertheless, the Samaritan Israelites deserve to be regarded as the true heirs of ethnic Israel for other reasons. These include, among the foremost, the superiority of the touchstones of the Samaritan Pentateuch, Mt. Gerizim, and other beliefs and practices over those held and practiced by these other Israelites. We should acknowledge that what we miss because of these evidentiary problems – especially in contrast to what survives in the Christian and even the Jewish cases – is a sense of the true variety of Samaritan Israelite ethnic expressions that likely characterized the actual experience of Samaritan Israelites in Late Antiquity. But I think the evidence still supports the view that biology plus was *a* major strategy already.

One reason I am so convinced even without explicit evidence is that if anything seems clear, it is that the Samaritan Israelite devotion to Gerizim as

---

[68] Indeed, this is another thing that they share with the Jews. It has been suggested that nearly a thousand years separates Josephus from the next surviving Jewish text that might be described as a *history*, the Sefer Josippon (Cohen, *The Jews in Late Antiquity*, 5). Yosef Hayim Yerushalmi is even more forbidding. After Josephus, he says, "it would be almost fifteen centuries before another Jew would actually call himself a historian (Yerushalmi, *Zakhor*, 16).

[69] These dates are found in Crown, "Samaritan Literature," 41–45. Pummer suggests similar dates – the tenth or eleventh centuries for Asatir, the Tulidah in the mid twelfth with later additions, the Kitab al-Tarikh in the fourteenth, the New Chronicle from around 1900, and Chronicle II in the early twentieth (Pummer, *The Samaritans*, 243–48).

a holy site was regarded by them as a unique feature of their identity well prior to Late Antiquity. In fact, it is more remarkable than is usually acknowledged that so much of the early evidence, no matter how limited, *makes* this perfectly clear – and much more so than is the case for the Jews and the Temple Mount in Jerusalem. This certainly includes some of the earliest relevant evidence, consisting of two dedicatory plaques from an apparent Samaritan Israelite synagogue on the island of Delos from as early as the third and second centuries BCE which were given in honor of donors by "the Israelites" who make offerings "on Mt Gerizim."[70] And, Mt. Gerizim appears in a very short account of a meeting between Jesus and a Samaritan Israelite woman in the New Testament, which is also the book in which the term "Samaritan" appears for the first time.[71] Here, in John 4, a Samaritan Israelite woman confronts Jesus saying, "our ancestors worshipped on this mountain," meaning Gerizim, "but you say ... people must worship ... in Jerusalem" (John 4:19). In context, the point of the story is that she mistakes him for a typical Jewish authority and he reveals himself as something else. But this encounter still shows that already, a particular devotion to Gerizim was so associated with Samaritan Israelite identity that it is almost the only thing that comes up in the conversation.

Turning to what literature there is from Late Antiquity, we quickly find that Gerizim maintains its salience. Again, we can really say very little about Samaritan Israelite self-understanding in this period, or even, really, about Samaritan Israelite history. We cannot even answer such questions as when the great religious reformer Baba Rabba, who is usually credited with giving Samaritan Israelite religion many of its distinctive features, actually lived although the third and fourth centuries CE seem most likely.[72] We can say that the community experienced waves of violence and repression throughout Late Antiquity, some initiated by various rebellions that were bloodily put down – in, at least, 484, 529, and 556. In addition, we see laws leveled against them during the reigns of the emperors Honorius and Arcadius in 404 CE, Valentinian in 426, and Theodosius II in 438.[73] At the same time, as Chalmers rightly observes, the tendency to characterize wide swathes of historical experience primarily as eras of "disaster" is a common one in studies of groups that

---

[70] Bruneau and Bordreuil, "Les Israélites de Délos et la juiverie délienne," 465–504; White, "The Delos Synagogue Revisited," 133–60.

[71] Meaning the New Testament, not John specifically. Jan Dušek suggests that it may have emerged as a companion term to "Ιουδαισμος," Judaism, which he claims appears for the first time in 2 Maccabees, "probably written in the 140s BCE" (Dušek, *Aramaic and Hebrew Inscriptions*, 81).

[72] Pummer, *The Samaritans*, 132–33.

[73] Pummer, *The Samaritans*, 135–37, 139, 141. Pummer further notes that the 426 law was "reissued, slightly revised, in 527 or 528 in *Codex Justinianus* 1.5.13" (136).

scholars consider "peripheral," fairly or not, and is to be avoided as a totalizing description.[74]

Again there are surviving compositions from this period and from a certain perspective – relative to many other groups – a considerable body thereof. The most important and influential, outside of the Samaritan Targum, are the Tibat Marqe and a body of oft-neglected Samaritan poetry. The former is a midrashic expansion on the Pentateuch attributed to Marqe who is most often supposed to have lived in the second half of the fourth century CE.[75] The latter consists of poems attributed to three third- and fourth-century poets, of whom Marqe himself is one. The others are his father Amram and his son Ninna. These were tremendously influential compositions. As Laura Lieber has observed in a recent edition of many of the poems, "[t]he writings of Amram, Marqe, and Ninna shaped the Samaritan liturgy as it existed throughout the Middle Ages and into the present" and "constitute a significant component of the Samaritan religious experience."[76]

The challenge of these texts is that they are not explicit about articulations of Samaritan Israelite identity. On some level, that is what is bracing about them to the *scholar* of identity: they are a helpful corrective to the tendency that has sometimes reigned in their study, the idea that they are always to be viewed in relation to the traditions of other groups. In other words, what these compositions do best is remind people that Samaritan Israelites did not, in fact, spend all of their time thinking about how they related to Jews or Christians. At the same time, they can also tell us that what was true of the Jews is true of the Samaritan Israelites, that they were a part of, rather than apart from Late Antiquity. Lieber notes how "Marqe's later writings reveal a specifically Samaritan understanding of the idea of the Logos," reflecting their situatedness in Late Antique intellectual culture, as well as how the "theology" of all three poets "anticipates concerns that are more fully developed in Islam ... insistent declarations that 'there is no God but the one' recur throughout the compositions by Amram Dare, Marqe, and Ninna."[77] And we should take a minute to note that this same embeddedness is what we saw in the prior consideration of the material remains of Jewish Late Antiquity, especially graffiti.

Still, in and of themselves, "Samaritan writings from late antiquity are largely 'inward' in orientation. They were written for use in religious worship and

---

[74] Chalmers, "The Rise and Fall of a Peripheral People?" 217–47.   [75] Tal, *Tibat Marqe*, 1.
[76] Lieber, *Classical Samaritan Poetry*, 14. More practically, she notes that while reconstructing the exact liturgy of this era is impossible, a collection of apparently typical readings was eventually created, called the Defter, and in it, two-thirds of the hymns are from these three individuals (Lieber, *Classical Samaritan Poetry*, 14–15).
[77] Lieber, *Classical Samaritan Poetry*, 19.

study, and ... they are less interested in issues such as boundary delineation."[78] In the case of the liturgical poetry, these are hymns that glorify God, distinguished from others largely by their frequent reference to Mt. Gerizim.[79] Central figures common to both Jewish and Samaritan Pentateuchs appear often, especially Moses and the patriarchs, but not the figures who, in later Samaritan Israelite tradition, divided the Jewish people from the Samaritan Israelites – Eli, or Ezra for example. As for Tibat Marqe, a six-book collection, Tal observes that "there is little doubt that only the first book was penned by Marqe himself," the others being written in the "language and style" of a much later period.[80] This "Book of Wonders" offers a vision of the exodus narrative full of specifically Samaritan Israelite concepts like the era of "Divine Favor" and "Disfavor."[81] But there are no clear statements in it attempting to distinguish the Samaritan Israelites from their rivals even in parts that recite the various historical calamities that might be used as a staging ground for critiques of other parts of Israel.[82]

What is useful about this corpus, then, is mainly what I have already said: that it at least clearly demonstrates the continued importance of the *exclusive* touchstones of Samaritan Israelite identity from earlier eras. And I think we can extrapolate that the inclusion of references to these touchstones was in part to emphasize the exclusive right of the Samaritan Israelites to an Israelite identity. In other words, the Samaritan Israelites would obviously have known the Jews did not consider Gerizim to be a holy site, and that their Pentateuch was different than the Jewish one, and they would have regarded themselves as superior Israelites on these and other grounds. They knew that Gerizim in particular was what made them unique. At the same time, these poems cannot be said to make any specific historical claims about the exclusivity of Samaritan Israelite claims to an Israelite identity in the way the Jewish texts I previously discussed did, so they are best used as suggestive evidence.

The question then indeed becomes whether the materials clearly from a later, and even much later period, can tell us anything about Samaritan Israelite

---

[78] Lieber, *Classical Samaritan Poetry*, 13.
[79] There may be ways to read polemic into this text. Stefan Schorch starts his short article on "Samaritan Perspectives on the Samaritan-Jewish Split" with a poem from Amram Dare, noting that its insistence on the primacy of the Torah, Moses, Mt. Gerizim, and Yahweh incapsulates both "the fundamental similarity between Judaism and Samaritanism" and "the most important and most contentious difference between the two rival groups – the localization of Israel's one holy mountain" (Schorch, "Woe to Those Who Exchanged the Truth for a Lie," 41).
[80] Tal, *Tibat Marqe*, 2–3. That is, it is written in fourth century Aramaic, "just like the poems that bear Marqe's name." In the rest, "[e]very period of the linguistic evolution of the Samaritan community left its traces," from Aramaic to Hebrew, to an artificial, literary Aramaic "mixed with Hebraisms" (Tal, *Tibat Marqe*, 5).
[81] Tal, *Tibat Marqe*, 37–39. [82] See, for example, Tal, *Tibat Marqe*, 45.

identifications in Late Antiquity, and here, I think there are two potential ways of answering the question. The first is to suppose that the texts in question simply *preserve* much older traditions. This they may well do, but we have no way of knowing, and I think the evidence for the fluidity of traditions over time, as a general rule, is too significant to assume it. The second, more practical in my opinion, is to suppose that the *strategy of ethnic identifying* they reflect – what I have called the "biology plus" strategy – is a *type* of the strategy that was already being employed in Late Antiquity, whether or not the individual stories that survive were the means through which it was deployed. This strategy is very different from the one we see in the Jewish texts I investigated, which generally relied on "foreignizing" the Samaritan Israelites and judging their potential inclusion mainly on the grounds that converts can be included.[83] But it may well have been commonly employed among Samaritan Israelites throughout Late Antiquity, and indeed, I think it likely was, for a number of reasons.

For one thing, the evidence, in my view, profoundly suggests that not just the Samaritan Israelites but their Israelite ancestors were long aware that there was an important distinction between an Israelite Israelite and a Judahite Israelite, which is to say, long before there were Jews or Samaritan Israelites. This view, it may be said, is in contradistinction to more typical understandings of Samaritan Israelite history and prehistory which, I have argued before, are overly influenced by what is really a "biblical claim rather than a demonstrated reality": that "all Israel" was more important throughout the biblical period than the reality of a divided Judah and Israel.[84] It is from this perspective that the typical "parting of the ways" paradigm emerges, in which the question is not only when these Israelites became Samaritan Israelites but when they fully disengaged from the people of Judah to become "other" Israelites in the first place. Before that, it is often assumed that Israelites and Judahites were embraced by what Pummer calls a "common Israelite tradition."[85] And in recent years, certain scholars have argued that a definitive break did not occur until even after the era of the early rabbis.[86]

Acknowledging that it is of course the case that later rabbinic texts tend to draw harder boundaries than earlier ones, I still think the evidence mainly suggests the existence of a constant awareness of difference from very early times.[87] This includes an early use of the biology plus strategy, this time in the Hebrew Bible itself, where it stands in dramatic contradistinction to the more

---

[83] For "foreignization" as an identity strategy in the ancient world, see Ballentine, "Foreignization in Ancient Competition," 18–36.
[84] Tobolowsky, *The Myth of the Twelve Tribes of Israel*, 71.
[85] Pummer, *The Samaritans*, 128. Weingart, "What Makes an Israelite an Israelite?" 163.
[86] Schiffman, "The Samaritans in Tannaitic Halakhah"; Lavee, "The Samaritan May Be Included," 147–73.
[87] See the discussion in Tobolowsky, *The Myth of the Twelve Tribes of Israel*, 80–81.

familiar biological strategy that appears in 2 Kings 17. The text in question is 2 Chronicles 30, another vision that, in my view, concerns the aftermath of the Assyrian conquest, where certain survivors from Israel actually come down to Jerusalem to have a unifying Passover celebration with their southern brethren under the leadership of the Judahite king Hezekiah.[88] The author of this Chronicles text, who therefore clearly acknowledges that there remained plenty of Israelites in Israel, instead disqualifies the northerners from primacy in Israel by repeated references to the inadequacy of their religious practices in contrast to those which reigned at the court of Hezekiah. In my previous study, I called this text "a masterpiece[e] of passive aggression," in the sense that it imaginatively depicts the *submission* of Israelites to a Judahite way of doing business.[89] But it also shows a clear awareness of already existing differences even in *ritual practices*. In other words, the northerners – already – apparently do not sanctify themselves before the meal in the same way or go through the process of eating it in the same way as the Judahites (2 Chron 30:17–18).

In addition, those who make the case for unity within Israel until a second- or third-century CE rupture have to go to some lengths to explain away the fact that in the early rabbinic period, hardly a century had passed since the Gerizim temple was *destroyed by Judahites* – by John Hyrcanus, Hasmonean leader of Judah, around 110 BCE.[90] Other pre-rabbinic texts might gesture towards a similar awareness of difference, including the book of Ben Sira, from the early second century BCE.[91] And even the relevant rabbinic texts often appear

---

[88] See the discussion in Tobolowsky, *The Myth of the Twelve Tribes of Israel*, 80–84. It certainly is not clear here that this event is set in the aftermath of the conquest, and the main clue is the fact that the invitation is sent to those Israelites "who have escaped from the hands of the kings of Assyria" (2 Chron 30:6). It would be possible to read this as a reference to some earlier invasion, and, as Sara Japhet has observed, 2 Chron 29 places the events it describes in the first year of Hezekiah while according to Kings the conquest happened in the sixth year of Hezekiah (2 Kings 18:10) (Japhet, "Exile and Restoration," 40). However, there are no more references to Hezekiah's regnal years in any of the rest of Chronicles' account of his reign and I see no reason to assume the events in 2 Chron 30 happened in the same year as 2 Chron 29 *or* that its authors necessarily share a chronological understanding with the authors of Kings. Japhet suggests the authors of Chronicles have conflated multiple invasions.

[89] Tobolowsky, *The Myth of the Twelve Tribes of Israel*, 81.

[90] Chalmers observes that the traditional dating of 129 BCE, from Josephus, has generally given way to 111/110 in recent scholarship because of numismatic evidence (Chalmers, "Samaritans, Biblical Studies, and Ancient Judaism," 37).

[91] Ben Sira 50:25–26: "My whole being detests two nations, while a third is not a nation at all: those who live on the mountains of Samaria, the Philistines, and the foolish people who live in Shechem." Schorch notes that this reference appears only in the Greek version of the text, while in the Hebrew version, Seir rather than Samaria is mentioned. He takes this to mean that the Samaritans rose to prominence in between the early and late 2nd BCE, which is when these two versions date from (Schorch, "The Construction of Samari(t)an Identity," 137). See also the discussion in Friedheim, "Some Notes," 193–202. Pummer, noting the absence of a reference to Gerizim in this text, suggests that it may not have originally referred to Samaritans (Pummer, *The Samaritans*, 49).

more *rhetorically* open than actually inclusive – especially in the sense, as I discussed previously, that they tend to oppose one pre-eminent rabbinic authority to another. It was Akiva who thought they were "true converts" and Ishmael who thought they were "lion converts", and Simeon ben Gamaliel who thought they were "like Israelites" and Judah ha-Nasi who thought they were "like gentiles." There is, then, always an awareness of a border of sorts, and it is constituted by a shared awareness of different beliefs, practices, and, indeed, mountains.

Thus, there is every reason to suppose that a biology plus strategy of ethnic identifying was already operational in Late Antiquity, and this view is additionally supported by a somewhat neglected aspect of the Jewish evidence that I discussed in the previous section. While there are indeed a great many discussions of whether, how, and how much to include Samaritan Israelites in the relevant Jewish texts, at least rhetorically, there are none that even suggest that the *Jewish* people had to defend themselves against Samaritan Israelite claims of "foreignization."[92] Instead, what there are, where confrontations between the rabbis and actual Samaritans are concerned, are texts like Genesis Rabbah 32:10. Here, Rabbi Jonathan has to refute a Samaritan Israelite who calls Gerizim a blessed mountain and Jerusalem a mountain of ruins, and further asserts that Gerizim was not covered by Noah's flood. While Rabbi Jonathan fails to have a ready response – because "the *halakha* ... was forgotten for a moment by Rabbi Jonathan" – his donkey driver notes that Genesis 7:19 claims that all the highest mountains were covered, so that either Gerizim was among these or else too pitiful to be noted by the biblical author. For this assistance, Rabbi Jonathan richly blesses him.[93]

In another telling passage, also from Genesis Rabbah (Gen. Rab 94:7), Rabbi Meir asks a Samaritan Israelite which tribe he descends from. The Samaritan Israelites responds that he is from the tribe of Joseph, which broadly accords with Samaritan Israelite traditions on the matter.[94] Meir demurs, the Samaritan Israelite asks him which then, and Meir responds that the Samaritan Israelite is from Issachar, since Shimron is mentioned in the Bible as one of the sons of Issachar. The Samaritan Israelite man goes to relate what he takes to be an exciting new discovery to the Samaritan Israelite patriarch. But the Samaritan Israelite patriarch observes, "from Joseph he has removed you, but he has not placed you in Issachar," meaning that Meir was not making a historical explanation but showing how easily Samaritan Israelite claims are confounded by rabbinic cleverness. In

---

[92] A term usefully developed in Ballentine, "Foreignization in Ancient Competition."
[93] Lieber, *Classical Samaritan Poetry*, 9–10.
[94] Even today, Samaritan Israelites identify according to the tribes of Manasseh, Ephraim, and Levi. There was also a Benjaminite family until 1968, for which, see Tsedaka, "Families."

both cases, the Jewish actor has to refute Samaritan Israelite claims to superiority, or merely belonging, vis-à-vis shared traditions and shared ancestry. No *defense* is needed because there do not appear to have been any weaponized Samaritan claims of Jewish foreignization. Meanwhile, to put it explicitly, the defenses there are, are consistent with the view that, already, Samaritan Israelites understood themselves to be Israelites who were distinguished from the Jews by having a different, superior set of cultural touchstones *despite* their shared ancestry and shared belonging in, for example, the tribal system.

The combination of these two recognitions – that it is indeed clear that there was a consciousness of the difference between Israelites and Judahites stretching backwards well into the biblical period, and that it *seems* clear that the Samaritan Israelites always acknowledged that the Jews were nevertheless descended from Israelites – is what makes the case that later stories at least reflect earlier strategies. After all, if there was a consciousness of the difference between the two groups it had to be articulated in some way, and there is no evidence of a Samaritan Israelite denial of Jewish Israelite heritage. Mostly likely, then, the typical strategy was already "biology plus." And since we have many examples of what that looks like from the chronicles, we may well suspect that earlier discourses *looked* the same, whether or not the same or similar stories were employed. So the "Samaritan Israelite Strategy," which is the biology plus strategy, was to explain in various ways how the Samaritans came to possess the superior beliefs, practices, scriptures, and holy mountain *despite* the fact that they and the Jewish people once formed a singular ethnic people Israel.

Treating the chronicles as examples of a type of strategy, then, what we see, for the most part, are a host of historical explanations as to how the two groups of Israelites came to be different and how the ancestors of the Jews consistently refused to be reconciled to Samaritan Israelite superiority. Consider, for example, well-known Samaritan Israelite traditions about Eli and Ezra. The former, here, is supposed to be the figure who began the corruption of Israelite practice that resulted in Judaism.[95] The latter, who in Nehemiah 8:1 is supposed to have read "the book of the *torah* of Moses" to the assembled community of Judahite returnees and has therefore often been associated with the completion of the Torah we know, is, instead, a mere thief who stole the Samaritan Israelite version and changed it, including by falsely elevating Jerusalem at the expense of Gerizim.[96] Fried also

---

[95] Pummer, *The Samaritans*, 2.
[96] More precisely, he removed references to Gerizim, since there are no references to Jerusalem in the Pentateuch. The idea of Ezra as corruptor is present in other religious traditions, including Islamic, for which see Fried, "Ezra among Christians, Samaritans, Muslims, and Jews of Late Antiquity," 118–47. Fried also observes that in 4 Ezra, Ezra receives a divine potion that allows him to dictate "the twenty-four books of the Hebrew Bible . . . as well as seventy secret texts that were to be revealed only to the wise" (Fried, *Ezra and the Law in History and Tradition*, 118).

mentions a Muslim chronicler of the tenth century, al-Mas'udi, who understood the Samaritans to believe that it was Zerubbabel who – accidentally – produced a false Torah by misremembering, at a time when the Judahites in Exile were attempting to reconstruct it *from* memory.[97] And if these are the most prominent examples of the biology plus strategy at work, there are many more.[98]

Another well-known account, this time from Chronicle II, offers a replay of the scene in 2 Chronicles 30, in which Hezekiah invites the Israelites to a Passover. In it, the Samaritan Israelite community is presented as already separate even from the rest of the Israelites, the latter of which are described as the "eight tribes."[99] This reflects one of the main ways Samaritan Israelites, since at least the era of the chronicles, have articulated their own Israelite identity to themselves – as the descendants, mainly of the tribes of Ephraim and Manasseh, with, as well, a Levitical lineage of priests of their own.[100] At any rate, in this story, even the eight tribes refuse to come but going on to the "Samaritan Israelites" the messengers are told that these will not "substitute evil for good and forsake the chosen place Mount Gerizim." The Samaritan Israelites invite Hezekiah to their Passover instead, the latter refuses, and "the people of Judah performed the Passover offering by themselves."[101]

Another story, which appears in slightly different forms in New Chronicle, the Samaritan Book of Joshua, and *Kitāb al-Tarikh*, is actually set in the Babylonian Exile, although in reality, only the Judahites were "Exiled."[102] Regardless, in all three of these accounts, when the time comes to return to Israel, each side invites the other to come with them and become, in the words of the Book of Joshua, "one word and one soul."[103] Naturally, in all of these accounts, neither group is interested in following the other's lead and the result is a public disputation before the Babylonian king between leaders of each community. In all three cases, the Judahite champion is Zerubbabel, who, in

---

[97] Fried, *Ezra and the Law in History and Tradition*, 125.
[98] See, generally, Schorch, "Woe to Those Who Exchanged the Truth for a Lie," 45–51. Schorch also mentions the presence of Samaritan Israelite versions of traditions about figures such as Adam, Enoch, Noah, Isaac and Jacob that link them to Mt. Gerizim in various ways – that, for example, Adam was supposedly created from its dust, that Isaac's attempted sacrifice took place there, and that Jacob saw his ladder there. Since some of these appear in Tibat Marqe, they are indeed Late Antique in origin and demonstrate that Late Antique Samaritan Israelites were in fact using a shared repertoire of traditions to draw boundaries between themselves and the Jewish people in "biology plus" terms (Tibat Marqe 2:44–50).
[99] Anderson and Giles, *Tradition Kept*, 251. See, also, the discussion in Tobolowsky, *The Myth of the Twelve Tribes of Israel*, 90–92.
[100] Knoppers, *Jews and Samaritans*, 20.   [101] Anderson and Giles, *Tradition Kept*, 251.
[102] "As far as we know, Samaria did not participate in the rebellions against King Nebuchadnezzar, and as a consequence most of its major towns did not experience the serious losses that Jerusalem and other major Judean urban centers experience in the early 6th century" (Knoppers, *Jews and Samaritans*, 121).
[103] Crane, *The Samaritan Chronicle*, 113.

Ezra 1–4, was the leader of the first Judahite "Return." While in the New Chronicle, the Samaritan champion is Abdiel the High Priest, in the Book of Joshua and the *Kitab*, it is "Sanballat the Levite." This is, presumably, the same Sanballat who, in the book of Nehemiah, frustrates Nehemiah's efforts to build the wall around Jerusalem. At any rate, what happens in the story is that both Pentateuchs are thrown in a fire but the Samaritan Pentateuch does not burn, proving its superiority.

This is the biology plus strategy in action. It offers a double move. First, it acknowledges that two groups indeed share biological ancestors and that both still identify primarily on the basis of that descent. Second, it advances the argument that, at one crucial point, their history went one way, ours another, rendering one group more legitimate than the other as heirs. We may not be able to tell how exactly this ethnic strategy was articulated in Late Antiquity but it seems tremendously likely that it was articulated, and it is likely enough, too, that the same repertoire of figures and events played a supporting role in these productions as it would in the later periods in which the chronicles were composed. After all, since it is clear that Gerizim and the Samaritan Pentateuch were understood by Samaritan Israelites as the markers of distinction that they actually are, there must have been stories about how one group of Israelites came to venerate them while another group went without from the beginning.

Then, where the more general goals of this study are concerned, what the Samaritan Israelite case study demonstrates is the validity of the principles I began with. Again, many scholars believe that traditions of shared descent, even fictive descent, are the sine qua non of ethnicity: the absolute, most basic requirement for calling something an ethnic identity. And it is true that many ethnic groups *do* present themselves as distinct from other groups because of an exclusive claim to descend, biologically, from an earlier group. This is clear even in the ancient world. Buell, too, notes that her departure from the norm on this topic is not intended to "minimi[ze] the prevalence of ancient appeals to kinship and descent in formulating claims of collective identity."[104] But, prevalent and necessary are not the same things.[105] And once again, the presence of multiple groups claiming to be the *same group* at once – "a world full of Israels" – helps reveal the weak links in the premise.

---

[104] Buell, *Why This New Race*, 9.

[105] "Most definitions of ethnicity acknowledge that other factors (language, religion, place, foodways) may be claimed by a given community as more central than kinship or descent. Nonetheless, when kinship and descent are privileged as necessary to ethnicity, these other factors are dismissed as mere 'markers' or attributes to ethnicity, rather than being ethnicity's constitutive elements" (Buell, *Why This New Race*, 9).

After all, it makes a great deal of sense that in a context where two groups who understand themselves to share biological descent – whether Jews and Samaritan Israelites, or Ethiopian Christians who claim Israelite descent and Beta Israelites, or Beta Israelites and Mormons, or whomever – end up competing over legacy, descent alone should come to seem like an insufficient quality for the making of ethnic subjects.[106] It just doesn't happen very often. And then, while the rhetorical move to claim that only one group really has this descent might seem like the natural one, this is only when we already assume that appeals to the authority of exclusive descent are the more natural way of constructing ethnic identities. When, however, we open our eyes to the possibility that the difference between the approaches of each group is not the difference between the natural, or normal, and the unnatural, but between two (or more) equally valid strategies, however more popular one is than the other, we are forced to concede *that* appeals to exclusive descent are a strategy like any other. And the last case study will further illustrate the point, by showcasing authors who presented themselves as ethnic Israelites while arguing that descent was an *irrelevant* feature of this identification.

Finally, what we see clearly here, which also prepares the way for the last discussion, is the evidence for the individuality and variety of ethnic expression – the "fixity and fluidity" Buell mentions, the difference between the starting points represented by received tradition and the actuality that they only appear where something is *being done* with them. Even though we do not have what we would like to have from Late Antiquity itself, it is still clear from later traditions that, here, too, there was no one way to navigate a received repertoire of figures and events to build boundaries. To say that there is a Samaritan Israelite strategy is to say that there is a typical *starting point*, *not* a consistent, or omnipresent, way of moving forward from there. What happened next, for whom, is something we have to imagine in this case, but this is not so difficult.

Christian Constructions of Israelite Identity in Late Antiquity

Early Christian literature, like early Jewish literature – like Gulliver among the Lilliputians – presents us with an immense and sprawling corpus. In the era I am interested in, this body has often been gathered up in the category called "Patristic literature," referring to the "Church Fathers," and anatomized from there. The famous Council of Nicaea of 325 provides one set of helpful dividing

---

[106] See the discussion in Tobolowsky, *The Myth of the Twelve Tribes of Israel*, 189–237. Generally speaking, Beta Israel traditions suggest that the Solomonic royal dynasty which was Christian, claimed to be Israelite, and ruled into the 1970s, lost their way when they converted.

lines between "Ante-Nicene," "post-Nicene," and for that matter "Nicene" Fathers. Languages provide another: "Greek," "Latin," or "Syriac" Fathers. Then there are other categories such as the "Apostolic Fathers," who worked in the period within living memory of the twelve apostles, or the "Desert Fathers," who lived in the Egyptian desert. And, of course, it bears noting that the whole category is imperfect, suggesting the exclusion of a number of women who contributed significantly to the intellectual foundations of the Church such as Melania the Elder and Paula of Rome.[107]

Obviously, anyone who wishes to address a particular aspect of this corpus must pick and choose and forgo, to some extent, the hope of a representative sample. My own interest, of course, lies in the operation of what I call the "abiological" strategy in this literature. In other words, I am interested in early Christian authors who not only claimed that Christians could be Israelites despite lacking biological descent from Israel but denied the relevance of descent altogether. This discourse is a subset of the one known to scholars of Christianity as the "Verus Israel," or "true Israel" discourse, which is usually held to have emerged in the work of Justin Martyr in the early second century. But both Verus Israel and aspects of the abiological strategy have roots of various sorts in earlier compositions such as the letters of Paul, the Letter to the Corinthians attributed (likely falsely) to Clement, and the Epistle of Barnabas. And, as with every discussion in this piece, the *variety* that attends its implementation in subsequent centuries is one of the strategy's most notable features. Certainly, we will see something of just how many different explanations for *why* Christians should be regarded as Israel there were, and of what the *significance* of being Israel could seem to be.

My intention, then, is to begin with the aforementioned roots and spend some time with Justin. From there, I will chart a wide course through the literary legacies of the (Ante-Nicene) Irenaeus of Lyon, Clement of Alexandria, and Cyprian of Carthage; to the likewise Alexandrian Origen and the likewise Carthaginian Tertullian; to Antony, the third- and fourth-century Desert Father; the fourth-century Ambrose of Milan; and the fourth- and fifth-century Augustine of Hippo. Next, I will discuss some figures whose divergent use of an inherited vocabulary of tradition helps illustrate the scope of what is really possible for an individual drawing on authorizing inheritances, specifically the third- and fourth-century Lactantius and the fourth-century Amphilochius of Iconium. And I will conclude with a consideration of Israel language among, and referring to, Christian groups such as the Marcionites, Donatists, and Manichaeans. This last

---

[107] For an insightful, feminist discussion of the construction of the category in scholarship, see Clark, *Founding the Fathers*.

exploration will not only help make the full picture of the operation of the abiological strategy more visible but facilitate discussion of an additional aspect of why Israelite identity was such an important topic in Christian intellectual output in the first half of the first millennium CE. In short, just as early Christians were competing with the Jewish people over the legacy of Israel, the "Verus Israel" discourse had an important role to play in differentiating Christians groups from each other.

Of course, I want to remind readers here that I am not only interested in this phenomenon for its own sake. Instead, I will continue to pursue, through it, a larger argument about what ethnicity is. The variety I mentioned previously will reinforce one aspect of this case, drawing attention once more to the role *individual creativity* plays in producing ethnic visions. As we will see, here too, ethnicity is not *a* strategy it is how a set of strategies are actually used by individual people in real world contexts. And there is just no telling what anyone might decide to use an existing ethnic strategy to do, *including* subverting familiar understandings of ethnic identity itself, as something biological. And this is where we meet the second crucial argument, about the general variety of ethnic strategies – which, in fact, this case study will help make abundantly clear.

Again, the situation is that scholars still commonly define ethnic identity, fundamentally, as a form of identity premised on a belief in shared biological descent. Obviously, the abiological strategy explicitly does not present Christian Israelite identity this way, and this is one reason that, as Buell has observed, it has been usual in scholarship to suppose that Christian Israelites are doing something different, in claiming it, than Jews and Samaritan Israelites. In other words, since an identity *cannot* be both abiological and ethnic, theirs must instead be something else, perhaps a "religious" identity.[108]

The opposite is also true, however. If "abiological" Christian claims are functionally the same as any others, then they will actually *demonstrate* that ethnic identities need not be premised on biological descent, just as Buell has argued.[109] And in fact, putting these three cases in conversation with each other is a way of making this absolutely clear. After all, taken individually, both Jewish and Samaritan Israelite claims may well seem to conform to the view that ethnicity is inherently biological in expression. Even together, as a pair,

---

[108] "We have failed to recognize the importance and functions of ethnic reasoning in early Christian self-definition largely because of how dominant modern ideas about race, ethnicity, and religion inform our approaches to and presuppositions about the meaning of those three terms" (Buell, *Why This New Race*, 5). Later, she adds "[t]he almost unanimous view that early Christians defined themselves over and against ethnic or racial specificity ... relies on an understanding of race/ethnicity as ascribed or fixed" (Buell, *Why This New Race*, 10).

[109] Again, a central point in Buell's work as well.

they may reinforce this impression, featuring, essentially, a competition over who is the superior *biological* descendant of the original group. Yet, as I noted, here we have not two but three groups who are claiming the same identity, using the same traditions, in roughly the same historical context, for many of the same reasons. Rather than seek an explanation for why one attempt is fundamentally different from the other two, we should instead acknowledge that it is the biological definition that is wrong. An "aboilogical" strategy is an ethnic strategy like any other, and one that makes a good deal of sense when competing with "biological" heirs. Which, in turn, indeed reveals that claiming an identity via exclusive biological descent is *also* a strategy, however much more familiar.

In addition, recognizing that Christian attempts to claim the identity Israel are also ethnic helps us make sense of a number of other claims I will investigate. It allows us, for example, to take Christian accounts of *rebirth* in Christ more literally.[110] Someone who thinks they can be literally reborn will naturally think they can change identities, whatever we think about the supposed immutability of ethnic identity in other cases. And while it is true that Late Antique Christians often understood themselves to be Christian *and* something else – Roman, or Gothic, or Gaulic – this, too, is not disqualifying.[111] A person may indeed have more than one identity of an ethnic character at once, or perhaps, more than one potential ethnic identity that is only realized as ethnic in certain contexts.[112]

We might, then, usefully begin by thinking of the abiological strategy, overall, as an attempted solution to a problem *of* identity that emerged quite early in the history of Christianity.[113] Christianity developed, of course, out of Judaism – or perhaps we might say, *with* Judaism – chiefly among people who regarded themselves as Jewish, and for whom Jewish scriptures and traditions were centrally important.[114] Very quickly, however, it developed from these roots into a predominantly "gentile" religion. Marcel Simon, who wrote the

---

[110] As Buell observes, this rebirth discourse "illustrates one central way in which Christians depicted Christianness simultaneously in terms of 'essence' and transformation" (Buell, *Why This New Race*, 3).

[111] Buell, *Why This New Race*, 31–32.

[112] A useful concept in this direction is Bernard Lahire's vision of the "plural actor," in Bernard Lahire, *The Plural Actor*. This is an idea that has already been applied to the study of Christian identity in Late Antiquity by Eric Rebillard who observes that "[n]ot only are religious identifies fluid, i.e., the boundaries between the different categories are permeable, but they are not necessarily activated in a given context, even when available" (Rebillard, "Material Culture and Religious Identity in Late Antiquity," 430). A person may feel that they are an Israelite in one context and something else in another – a plural identity – without noticing any slippage.

[113] This "problem" language is also the language used by Marcel Simon; see Simon, *Verus Israel*, 69. This study was initially published in 1948, in French.

[114] Again, my view is that many of the familiar aspects of Judaism and Samaritanism emerged in the third and second centuries BCE, while Christianity debuted in the first century CE, an appreciably long time later. However, other key elements of Judaism as we know it did not emerge until after the destruction of the Temple in 70 CE, and there are ways in which they

classic treatment of Verus Israel in 1948, suggests that "Christians of gentile derivation made up by far the greater part of the church" already by the mid-second century and this is an inequality that would only accelerate.[115] In the Roman world, by the year 300, there were not only "Christian magistrates," there were "Christian governors of provinces, specially excused participation in pagan sacrifices."[116] And if Late Antiquity more or less began with a sudden explosion of violence and repression against Christians – the so-called "Great Persecution" of Diocletian – the early decades of the fourth century saw a string of developments that placed Christianity ever more at the center of the Roman world.[117] Which meant, in some ways, ever farther away from its original roots.

Naturally, the question was what to *do* with these roots in this brave, new Gentile world. It was still true, after all, that Jesus himself had been a follower of the Jewish faith. It was still true that the scriptures which would come to be known, in Christianity, as the Old Testament were venerated by many Christians and that their protagonist was Israel. It was still true that the biblical prophets spoke of Israel, that biblical promises were to Israel, and that Israel was known, in the Bible and in other traditions, as God's chosen people.[118] Different Christian groups would approach this problem differently, including those like the Marcionites, discussed shortly, who argued that Christianity should reject its Jewish roots as completely as possible. And there would also be those who found ways to argue that the Christians, as Christians, had actually been the intended recipient of biblical promises from the beginning, even sometimes the recipients of a revelation older than the Mosaic law. But certainly, we can think of the claim that the Christian people were the true Israelites – or, more often, that they had become the true Israelites because the Jews had forfeited the title –

---

are indeed simultaneous reactions to new realities, for which, see various essays in the volume Becker and Reed, *The Ways That Never Parted*. Christine Shepardson observes that "[i]dentifying John the Baptist, Jesus, and Paul as apocalyptic Jews places them more comfortably in their own context" and argues that "[t]he Roman destruction of the Jewish temple in Jerusalem CE marked a turning point in all of the biblical traditions that reconstituted themselves afterwards: Pauline and gnostic forms of gentile 'Christianity' flourished in the aftermath, as did the newly developing rabbinic traditions of Judaism" (Shepardson, "Christianity Emerges," 3–4).

[115] Simon, *Verus Israel*, 68.
[116] Chadwick, "The Early Church," 8.
[117] Schott, *Christianity, Empire, and the Making of Religion in Late Antiquity*, 1–2. Brown describes the years between 260 and 302 as an era of "complete tolerance" – sometimes called the "Little Peace of the Church" (Brown, *Late Antiquity*, 68). The early fourth-century events I refer to include the possibility of Constantine's conversion around the time of his victory at the Battle of Milvian Bridge in 312, the Edict of Milan, pronounced by him and Licinius and promulgating tolerance in 313, the first Council of Nicaea, which produced the famous "Nicene Creed" in 325, and Theodosius' "Edict of Thessalonica," which asserted the emperor's interest in establishing the primacy of "orthodox" Christianity throughout the Roman Empire, in 380.
[118] Simon, *Verus Israel*, 69–70.

as one way of solving the problem of an increasingly widespread Christianity, built on an Israelite foundation.

Given this, it can hardly be surprising that elements at least anticipating this discourse indeed appear already in the work of the apostle Paul, the famous "apostle to the Gentiles." To be sure, in various places, Paul seems to understand biological Israel to have retained a special status of sorts. He certainly emphasizes the importance of his own identity as an Israelite by birth: in Romans 11, "an Israelite, a descendant of Abraham, and a member of the tribe of Benjamin" (Romans 11:1), and in Philippians 3, "a member of the people of Israel, of the tribe of Benjamin, a Hebrew born of Hebrews; as to the law, a Pharisee" (Phil 3:5).[119] And in Romans 11, he seems to consider the Jewish people to have greater spiritual potential, as an Israel, than the gentiles. Here, we see his famous image of the olive tree, which represents God's people. He warns that if gentile converts have genuinely been grafted on as "wild olive shoots" while many Jews are "branches broken off," because of their refusal of Jesus's revelation, even so, he charges, "do not boast over the branches" broken off, "for if you have been cut . . . and grafted . . . how much more will these natural branches be grafted back into their own olive tree?" (11:17–18, 24).[120]

At the same time, Paul is quite clear in other places that the gentiles can become "an Israel of God" – and even seems to feel that becoming Israel, in this sense, is a necessary prerequisite for inheriting Israel's promises.[121] He anticipates later Christian authors by reading into the Hebrew Bible's stories certain supposed hints about the later status of gentile Christians, in, for example, the story of Isaac, Rebecca, and their children. He refers to the biblical narrative in Genesis 25:23 where YHWH tells Rebecca that two nations are in her womb, but the older will serve the younger (9:12). He argues explicitly that it is the "children of the promise" rather than "the children by physical descent" who are God's children and suggests that Christianity, being the younger religion, will step into that role.

Overall, however, what seems to be the case here is that Paul actually regarded the connection between gentile Christians and Israel to be at least quasi-biological in nature, via a transformation that occurred upon being embraced in the new covenant that Jesus inaugurates – through, among other things, the

---

[119] Jennifer Eyl has made a crucially important argument, drawing on these claims – that Paul was a rhetorician engaged in convincing different audiences of different things (Eyl, "I Myself Am an Israelite," 148–68). As a result, we should not necessarily expect intellectual consistency throughout his works.

[120] Staples observes that "thirteen of the nineteen uses of Israel/Israelite" in the letters most often considered authentically Paul's appear in Romans 9–11 (Staples, *Paul and the Resurrection of Israel*, 69).

[121] Thiessen, *A Jewish Paul*, 95. See also Novenson, *Paul and Judaism*.

intercession of *pneuma*, a new spirit.[122] Staples has a lengthy discussion of Paul's views on Gentile inclusion in Israel, noting how prior interpreters had often avoided it by sidestepping how clear it is that the biblical prophecies Paul intentionally echoes refer exclusively to Israel.[123] In his view, Paul draws on various Hebrew Bible proof texts "to present his gospel as the fulfilment of the promises to Israel in the wake of Israel's disobedience," because Israel's disobedience broke the covenant that made the promises possible. To restore the covenant and make fulfilment possible, "God will solve that problem with the Torah written on the heart ... the new heart and the new spirit," which will, in a sense, be biologically Israelite.[124] Others have made similar cases, including Paula Fredriksen, who sees Paul making a point that is similar to one we saw certain rabbinic authors making, that "gentile inclusion ... had already been promised to Abraham *through Christ* (Galatians 3:17)" – and Matthew Thiessen who argues that Paul believes "'if you are [part] of the Messiah [*ei hymeis Christou*], then you are the seed [*sperma*] of Abraham.'"[125]

We do, therefore, have to look later for the origins of the abiological strategy proper, which, again, seems to have first achieved its full and explicit expression in the work of Justin Martyr, born around 100 CE. There were other "roots," as I called them. Before Justin, the author of Clement's *Letter to the Corinthians* – again, an anonymous letter likely falsely ascribed to Clement I, bishop of Rome – seems to be entirely convinced, already, that the gentile Church is Israel. Indeed, Graham Harvey suggests that the author shows no awareness that Israel *could* be anyone else.[126] Instead, they refer to Israel as "the portion of God," describing how Jacob in particular became that portion "and Israel the lot of his inheritance" (1 Clement 29). Then, as they put it, "seeing, therefore, that we are the portion of the Holy One, let us do all those things which pertain to holiness" (1 Clement 30).[127]

Likewise, there was the Epistle of Barnabas, which, as Michael Kok observes, is an extremely early attempt to position "the Christian community as a people or nation in direct continuity with the revered texts of Israel, but with Judaism positioned as an adversarial foil."[128] In its author's view, the Jews, meaning the Israelites, had already lost "the covenant" in the days of Moses,

---

[122] Thiessen, *A Jewish Paul*, 98; Staples, *Paul and the Resurrection of Israel*, 175–76.
[123] Staples, *Paul and the Resurrection of Israel*, 75–77, 110–11.
[124] Staples, *Paul and the Resurrection of Israel*, 161–62.
[125] Fredriksen, *Paul: The Pagans' Apostle*, 106; Thiessen, *A Jewish Paul*, 95–97. See also Hodge, *If Sons, Then Heirs*.
[126] Harvey, *The True Israel*, 251.
[127] Translations here, and unless otherwise noted elsewhere, are from the collection *The Complete Works of the Church Fathers* edited by Philip Schaff. In this case, see Schaff, ed., *The Complete Works*, 17094.
[128] Kok, "The True Covenant People," 83. For Kok's discussion of dating issues, see Kok, "The True Covenant People," 87–88.

who symbolized the breaking of it by destroying the tablets at Sinai (Barnabas 4).[129] The author's extensive critique offers many reasons why these Israelites were never worthy of it and why it always belonged to the Christians.[130] The original Israel's "failings" serve for him "as a warning against complacency," as well as a sign of the wickedness of its contemporary heirs and their ancestors.[131] Overall, and drawing on Buell, Kok concludes that the author used "ethnic reasoning to carve out a place for the new Christian *genos* in the context of the Graeco-Roman world." In order to give deep roots to what was really a new phenomenon, "he completely appropriated the covenant, ancestors, and scriptures of Israel and simultaneously denied the legitimacy of the Judaean claim on these same scriptural traditions."[132] This preoccupation with covenant in particular, also present in the work of Paul, was a consistent early means of justifying the arrival of a new Israel, but it is interesting to note how often various Christian authors actually denied that the original Israelites had ever been true Israelites at all.

As for Justin himself, he does go farther and is more explicit, as the context of his *Dialogue with Trypho* – a real or imagined debate with a Jewish interlocutor – positions him to be. Throughout this dialogue, Justin offers many different explanations not only for why Christians are the true Israel but how the Jews have lost this title to them, in many cases through the kind of interpretive reading practice we have seen in the letters of Paul.[133] Above all, he repeatedly makes versions of the claim that "[w]e have been led to God through this crucified Christ, and we are the true spiritual Israel, and the descendants of Judah, Jacob, Isaac, and Abraham, who, though uncircumcised, was approved and blessed by God" (Dialogue 11).[134]

Perhaps the clearest expression of Justin's views occurs when the aforementioned Trypho asks the question directly: "Do you mean to say that you are Israel, and that God says all this about you?" (Dialogue 123)[135] After ridiculing Trypho for failing to get the point until then, Justin responds by paraphrasing Isaiah 44:

> in Isaiah, God, speaking of Christ in parable, calls him Jacob and Israel. This is what he says: Jacob is my servant, I will uphold him; Israel is my elect. I will put my spirit upon him and he shall bring forth judgment to the Gentiles ... Therefore, as your whole people was called after that one

---

[129] Schaff, *The Complete Works*, 14998.   [130] Kok, "The True Covenant People," 92–93.
[131] Rhodes, "The Two Ways Tradition," 810–11.   [132] Kok, "The True Covenant People," 93.
[133] Thomas B. Falls points to the possibility that this was "to reinforce a Christian readership in its belief that it had superseded the Mosaic Law and supplanted Judaism as the New Israel" as well as that "it was primarily addressed to Gentiles who were leaning toward Judaism" (Martyr, *Dialogue with Trypho*, xiii).
[134] Martyr, *Dialogue with Trypho*, 21.   [135] Martyr, *Dialogue with Trypho*, 185.

Jacob, surnamed Israel, so we who obey the precepts of Christ, are, through Christ who begot us to God, both called and in reality are, Jacob and Israel and Judah and Joseph and David and true children of God.[136]

Later he adds:

> When Scripture says, *I am the Lord God, the Holy one of Israel, who showed Israel your king,* will you not admit that Christ the eternal king is meant? For you know that Jacob, the son of Isaac, was never king ... Is it, therefore, in the patriarch Jacob and not in Christ, that you and the former Gentiles trust? As Christ is called Israel and Jacob, so we, hewn out of the side of Christ, are the true people of Israel. (Dialogue 135).[137]

Finally, echoing Paul, he concludes "that there were two seeds of Judah, and two races, as there are two houses of Jacob: the one born of flesh and blood, the other of faith and the Spirit" (Dialogue 135).[138] The latter, of course, is superior. And crucially, Justin is here going beyond Paul to the idea that there is – henceforth and forever – only *one* true Israel, that this conclusion was intended by Old Testament authors themselves, and that the Israel of faith is superior to the Israel of blood.

For us, the significance of Justin's argument for the debate about Israelite identity among Christians actually lies in two different directions. First, that it is indeed a watershed moment in the development of the abiological strategy that I am interested in here. But, as Buell observes, the mere fact that Justin is debating a Jewish interlocutor about who is the real Israel also *shows that he understands both the new and the old Israelite identities* in the same terms – which is to say, in both cases, in fundamentally ethnic terms. As Buell puts it, "Justin does not reject but rather redefines the concept of ethnoracial membership for Christians."[139] He does understand ethnicity as an expression of "an ethnoracial essence (something 'fixed')," just as most ethnic actors do today, and he understands those who share that essence as constituting a distinct "people," an ethnic group, as it were.[140] But he simply thinks the essence is something *other than what most people think the essence is today*. There is something about this, it may be said, in Paul's views on *pneuma* as well, but here, too, Justin is clearer and more explicit. He argues "that his Jewish interlocutors mistake flesh and blood for the correct essence of faith, spirit, and obedience to God."[141] In this, Justin is saying that "faith, spirit, and obedience to God" can be the essence of an ethnic identity. And I think we can follow

---

[136] Martyr, *Dialogue with Trypho*, 185–86.   [137] Martyr, *Dialogue with Trypho*, 203.
[138] Martyr, *Dialogue with Trypho*, 204.   [139] Buell, *Why This New Race*, 98.
[140] Buell, *Dialogue with Trypho*, 98.   [141] Buell, *Dialogue with Trypho*, 98.

by acknowledging that, in the premise at least, he is actually quite correct: ethnic identity does not need to be defined by descent or fictive descent; it can be defined by something else.

Next, between the time of Justin and the start of Late Antiquity, a number of different Christian intellectuals had different explanations for why Christians had succeeded to the place of Israel, either literally as Israel or simply as the heir of divine promises. From the mid-second to the mid-third century, for example, Irenaeus (Against Heresies 4.36.2), Clement of Alexandria (*Paedagogus* (2.8), and Cyprian of Carthage (*The Lord's Prayer*) all charted slightly different courses. For Irenaeus, it was the Jewish rejection of Jesus himself that caused God to "rejec[t] them, and giv[e] to the Gentiles outside the vineyard the fruits of his cultivation." Clement writes of how the (supposed) Jewish use of the crown of thorns had made gentiles into the likeness of the crown "who once were barren but are placed around Him through the Church of which He is the Head," while the Jewish people had "forfeited the place of the true Israel." For Cyprian, it was the crucifixion itself that brought about the replacement of God's prior people with a new one.[142] In his Treatise on the Lord's Prayer, he argued, reflecting on its famous opening, that the Jews "cannot now call God their Father, since the Lord confounds and confutes them" for rejecting and putting Jesus to death, referring to both John 8:44 and Isaiah 1:3 as proof texts.[143]

Then there were the likes of Origen and Tertullian, who, among their many intellectual legacies, not only put their own spin on the abiological strategy but developed useful tools for others to do so in still additional ways.[144] This they did by evolving further the existing tendency to read into the Hebrew Bible various proofs that the Christians were *always* intended to supplant the Jews as God's chosen people. Tertullian was another who saw an explicit reference to Judaism and Christianity in the promise to Jacob that the older should serve the younger, arguing that

> since the *people* or *nation* of the Jews is anterior in time, and "greater" through the grace of primary favour in the law, whereas ours is understood to be "*less*" in the age of times ... beyond doubt, through the edict of the divine utterance, the *prior* and "*greater*" people – that is, the Jewish – must necessarily serve the "*less*" ... that is, the Christian.[145]

---

[142] Schaff, *The Complete Works*, 26567–68, 16208.
[143] Schaff, *The Complete Works*, 18541–42.
[144] Tertullian was older by some decades but seems to have converted to Christianity around the turn of the century. See the brief biography in Dunn, *Tertullian*, 2–8.
[145] Schaff, *The Complete Works*, 43493.

This he paired with the view that Christian revelation itself went back all the way to Adam and that biological Israel had lost its way already in the days of the golden calf, showing the flexibility of past-oriented authority claims.[146]

As for Origen, he was so far devoted to the enterprise of looking for hidden references to Christian revelation that he compares those capable of divining the true Christian meaning of these texts to "the levites and priests" in the original biblical order, and those who are even better at it than others to the high priests.[147] Indeed, he defended this form of supersessionist exegesis explicitly against rabbinic reading practices, which he was unusually familiar with – though this is not to say that he got them right here. In other words, it was his view that in rabbinic circles, text is "not understood in its spiritual sense, but is interpreted according to the bare letter" (4.2.2) whereas his was the proper, spiritual reading.[148] In reality, as Wollenberg observes, "[t]he early rabbinic relationship with the Bible is often *treated* as the exemplar par excellence of . . . faithful reading practice" but the rabbis, too, "imagined the biblical text as . . . an echo of greater truths that had been cut off from the divine" and needed to be recovered as we have amply seen.[149] But in any case, Origen was an explicit proponent of the abiological strategy in a way that actually echoes the work of Philo mentioned previously.[150] In his *On First Principles*, Origen, too, argues that "Israel" is a term that means "one who sees God," belonging to whoever came closest to accurately understanding the nature of divinity (On First Principles 4.22).[151] He, therefore, not surprisingly argues that it was the failure to recognize Jesus that had cost the Jews their prerogative. In Origen's view, they literally did not "see God" when he arrived.[152] He makes a similar claim in

---

[146] Schaff, *The Complete Works*, 43494–95. Andrew Jacobs has noted to me that this argument appears already in the *Epistle of Barnabas*, which Tertullian may have been aware of (personal communication).

[147] Schaff, *The Complete Works*, 40688. For other discussions of Origen's relationship to Jewish practices and beliefs, and other reflections of this discourse, see Niehoff, "Circumcision as a Marker of Identity," 89–123; Drake, "Origen Reads Jewishness," 38–58. For some of Origen's own views, see generally First Principles 4.2.1–9; 4.3.1–5.

[148] As translated in Graves, "Origen," 71.   [149] Wollenberg, *The Closed Book*, 2.

[150] On the impact of Origen's Alexandrian upbringing, see Drake, "Origen Reads Jewishness," 38. A second important figure bringing ideas like Philo's into the mix was another Alexandrian, the slightly older Clement, for which see Runia, "Clement of Alexandria," 256–76.

[151] See Schaff, *The Complete Works*, 39860–61. As Drake also notes, Origen here embraces and forwards Paul's view of the difference between "Israel according to the flesh," "whom he identifies as 'God's former people,'" and "Israel according to the Spirit" – although she also thinks he goes beyond Paul and falsely attributes his more expansive view of this distinction to the authority of the earlier author (Drake, "Origen Reads Jewishness," 49). See *On First Principles* 4.1.4, 4.3.6, and Commentary on Romans 6.12.6 and 6.12.9. Later in *On First Principles* 4.23.

[152] Origen argues that "if then, there are certain souls in this world who are called Israel" than since "our Saviour came to gather together the lost sheep of the house of Israel; and as many of the Israelites did not accept His teaching, those who belonged to the Gentiles were called. From

Against Celsus, and in his *Commentary on the Book of John* he discovers in that book the view that "those who have believed in Christ, for they also, even if their bodily descent cannot be traced to the seed of the Patriarchs, are yet gathered out of the tribes."[153] Of course, this is an explicit account of the abiological strategy, tied, as with Justin, to the idea that the Israelite *ethnos* has different contents than in the biological strategy: spirit and faith rather than birth and blood. But, being premised differently as an argument, it also helps to show just how many different forms the same strategy can take in the hands of different authors.

Turning to Late Antiquity proper, we see the same dimensions of intellectual variety and individual creativity at play. There were, for example, those like Antony the Great, Ambrose of Milan, and Augustine of Hippo, all of whom also charted somewhat different courses from each other to, essentially, the same point. Antony, another Egyptian, made his case – as far as we can see it – in a way that reflects the influence of Alexandrian philosophy. This is in itself an important recognition. While the traditional image of Antony, as produced especially by Athanasius's *Life of Antony*, is of a saintly and simple man, Samuel Rubenson argues that the philosophical complexity of his surviving letters, seven in all, is itself a major reason to regard them as authentic.[154] But in Antony, we see still another dimension of the abiological strategy. Drawing on a host of ideas we have seen expressed in various ways already – the idea, for example, of Moses as the founder of the *spiritual* church, and the adoption of Christians into it (2:7, 10), and the idea that the name Israel means "a mind that sees God" (3:6) – he makes the case that his Christian flock has, in a sense, received new Israelite *souls*.[155] And the significance of this fact, for him, is that this is why they can expect to receive eternal life after death. We see this especially in letters 5, 6, and 7 where he refers to his addressees as "holy Israelites in their spiritual essence" and in letter 2 where he quotes Luke 2:34's blessing of Mary by Simeon, who says that Jesus would cause "the falling and rising of many in Israel" (2:33). In Antony's interpretation, this apparently means that the failure to embrace Jesus caused the "falling" of many *biological* heirs of Israel after *death*, and the "rising" of *spiritual* heirs of Israel,

---

which it will appear to follow, that those prophecies which are delivered to the individual nations ought to be referred rather to the souls" (On First Principles IV. 23) (Schaff, *The Complete Works*, 39863).

[153] For a more modern translation of the relevant part of *Contra Celsum*, see Origen and Chadwick, *Origen*, 72. For the passage from the commentary, see Schaff, *The Complete Works*, 40687.

[154] Rubenson, *The Letters of St. Antony*, 10–13, 35–45. He suggests they were written in the 340s, for reasons including Antony's apparent reference to his own mortality in the sixth letter (Rubenson, *The Letters of St. Antony*, 44).

[155] Rubenson, *The Letters of St. Antony*, 69. For a description of the Platonic, rather than Philonic, origins of Antony's doctrine of the soul and body, see Rubenson, *The Letters of St. Antony*, 61–64.

whomsoever they may be, to eternal life.[156] But, throughout we get the sense that his view is that the soul has become Israelite, through faith, and this has purchased eternal life for his flock. As he puts it in letter five: "I do not need to call you by your names in the flesh, which are passing away, for you are Israelite children" (5:1–2).[157]

As for Ambrose, in his "Explanation of Psalm 36," he appears to feel that Israel enjoyed what Gerda Heydemann calls an "exclusive claim to the status of chosen people" only so long as they were also a *separate* people.[158] In other words, "[t]he distinction between the people of God and the other peoples became blurred when Israel started to worship foreign gods and God retaliated by electing a new people, the Church, from among those previously considered unworthy."[159] In addition, in making his case that the Christians had now succeeded to their position, Ambrose, too, makes an explicitly ethnographic argument. He acknowledges that most ethnic groups usually take their names from the places where they live but presents the Christians as special for *being* defined by their faith as the "people of Christ."[160] In other words, he is perfectly aware that there are more common definitions of what passes for ethnic identity than the one he is advancing but sees no barrier to advancing it anyway.

Then, where Augustine, the one-time Manichaean and fourth and fifth century Bishop of Hippo is concerned, he followed Origen in his belief in the efficacy of the serious study of the Old Testament as Christian revelation for forming identity conceptions, as Paula Fredriksen has clearly laid out. For him, the Mosaic law "*was* the gospel," which is why, he thought, Paul praised the Jews for having it (*Against Faustus 12.3, 22.6*).[161] And he believed that Jesus was the fulfilment of all the various biblical references to sacrifice, obviating the need for any further ones.[162] As a result, he was, quite naturally, an intellectual heir of Paul: his vision of an "all Israel" to be redeemed, which Paul refers to in Romans 11:25–26, was not "all of fleshly Israel" but instead "the community of the elect, that tiny minority," who would "comprise the citizenry" of his city of God.[163] In other words, they stand apart from fleshly Israel because they are a different kind of Israel, but no less valid for all that.

---

[156] See, generally, Rubenson, *The Letters of St. Antony*, 203–205.
[157] Rubenson, *The Letters of St. Antony*, 212.
[158] Heydemann, "People(s) of God?" 37. See Ambrose, *Explanation on 12 Psalms*, 74–75.
[159] Heydemann, "People(s) of God?" 37. Ambrose, Explanation on Psalm 36, 6.
[160] Heydemann, "People(s) of God?" 37.
[161] Fredriksen, *Augustine and the Jews*, 233. Simon notes that he also makes a distinction between "carnal sonship" and "spiritual sonship" that allowed the Christians to be the true spiritual heirs of biblical figures like Abraham, or Jacob, and therefore the recipients of the actual promises made in biblical texts to their various progeny (Simon, *Verus Israel*, 148). See Augustine Ep. 196, 3, 13.
[162] Fredriksen, *Augustine and the Jews*, 250. [163] Fredriksen, *Augustine and the Jews*, 364.

Israel and Its Heirs in Late Antiquity

Where this discussion is concerned, Augustine's work is additionally useful because he offers a number of textbook examples of what Buell describes as the general Christian tendency to use "culturally available understandings of human difference" to make ethnic cases, which is to say, the tendency to redeploy difference language that already existed to draw ethnic boundaries.[164] In Heydemann's particularly insightful treatment, she shows Augustine navigating his way through a traditional Latin vocabulary for articulating peoplehood, especially the term "gens," which is often used to mean something more like an ethnic group, and "populus," which can be bound together by other things like laws. In the *City of God*, she argues, Augustine views the Israelites as a "gens" in the sense of shared descent, but also a "populus" in the sense that they were bound together by a divine mission.[165] "The establishment of the covenant between God and the Israelites through Moses on Mount Sinai" made them into a populus, "a people defined by their obedience towards divine law," despite having already, and also, been a gens.[166] As a result, Augustine argues – here at least – that the Christians could become the new *populus* Israel, whether or not they could become the *gens* Israel, by becoming faithful observers of the correct law. But, Christians could also think of themselves as part of a *gens* in the sense "that they could think of themselves as citizens in the heavenly Jerusalem." Thus, in Heydemann's words, "Augustine linked membership in the gens with notions not of common descent, but rather of citizenship and civic identity," and once again, descent becomes irrelevant for identifying who is really Israel.[167] Once again, too, the author is best understood not as advancing an argument for a different kind of identity for Christians *than* ethnic but as claiming that an ethnic identity can have different contents than expected.

Overall, then, when we survey these various instances of the abiological strategy both in Late Antiquity and before, we do indeed see what I have argued from the beginning. First, we see how an inherited strategy of ethnic identifying can serve as a starting point for any number of acts of ethnic boundary-making. But we also see that each attempt to employ that strategy will ultimately reflect the individual apprehensions, interests, and arguments of particular authors. It would be a mistake to think that the strategy exists apart from its application, because it is a mistake to think of ethnic identity as having that level of real, objective existence. But, the abiological strategy is indeed a shared beginning of many different ways of drawing ethnic boundaries.

At the same time it is when we turn to the bigger picture that we can really get a sense of how the case of Christian Israel advances my larger arguments.

---

[164] Buell, *Why This New Race*, 1–2.   [165] Heydemann, "People(s) of God?" 39.
[166] Heydemann, "People(s) of God?" 39.   [167] Heydemann, "People(s) of God?" 41.

Certainly, we see just how fluid and individual attempts to make identity can be, even when premised on broadly the same set of inherited traditions. There were, for example, a wide variety of Christian ways of navigating the biblical past, some of which had nothing, or little, to do with being Israel. We can consider Eusebius, the famous Church historian, who made the argument in the early fourth century CE that Abraham himself, well before Moses, had actually been the first recipient of Christian revelation (Eusebius HE 1.4). Thus, he argues that Jesus' doctrine was neither "new" nor "strange." Instead, "our life and our conduct, with our doctrines of religion, have not been lately invented by us, but from the first creation of man, so to speak, have been established." He added that those who "assert that all those who have enjoyed the testimony of righteousness, from Abraham himself back to the first man, were Christians in fact if not in name ... would not go beyond the truth."[168]

In this case, of course, Christians would neither need to be Israel nor to have succeeded Israel in some way because, instead, their revelation would actually be older than that of the Jewish people. And, as usual, other Christian authors, both before and after Eusebius, would make the same *kind* of argument using different figures: Melchizedek, or even Adam.[169] Indeed, Buell notes that "[f]ollowers of Christ regularly defined themselves as descendants of key figures such as Abraham (Paul, Justin, Pseudo-Clementine *Recognitions*), Seth (*Gospel of the Egyptians, Apocryphon of John*)," and, of course, "Jesus (Aristides' *Apology*, Justin's *Dialogue with Trypho*)."[170] As she astutely observes, the value of making a genealogical claim to greater authority in particular – which is part of why ethnic identity itself is so often presented as a genealogical fact – is that it does the work ethnicity is supposed to do. Since genealogies "offer a central way of communicating a sense of ethnic/racial 'fixity,' essence, and continuity," which, nevertheless, can be adapted to become more useful, they incapsulate the tension between fixity and fluidity Buell identifies.[171]

Meanwhile it is again the situation, as in the first section, that even though there were common ways of privileging certain parts of an inherited repertoire in the identity-making business, there were also those who did not stick to the common path but innovated through what was available and neglected. In this direction, we can consider, as an example, the work of Amphilochius, Bishop of Iconium in the late fourth century CE. In his "Against Heretics," as Andrew

---

[168] Schaff, *The Complete Works*, 19547–48. For a discussion of Abraham's importance in discourses that elevated the Christians above the Jews, see Siker, *Disinheriting the Jews*.

[169] Simon, *Verus Israel*, 80–86. He notes that it is "the Syrian author of the Cave of Treasures" who claimed Adam as the ancestor of Christian priesthood.

[170] Buell, *Why This New Race*, 76.   [171] Buell, *Why This New Race*, 75.

Israel and Its Heirs in Late Antiquity 49

Jacobs observes, he "creates a novel comparison between the objects of his treatise and the Samaritans."[172] In other words, he goes against type to use "Samaritan" rather than "Jew" or "Israelite" or any other term to make his argument, which is, in short, that the heretics that are the subject of his treatise are *symbolically* Samaritan Israelites in the sense that their refusal of true Christianity is like Samaritan Israelite refusal in Jewish traditions.

> Who doesn't recognize the Samaritans among us? Those who have turned away from Jerusalem – that is, Christ's Church – who have established a law no longer to offer prayer or first-fruits to God in Jerusalem, nor to heed the Scriptures or the teachings which have been given in the churches, to the shepherds from the holy spirit. (17)

Thus "just as the Samaritan through habit produced apostasy and was refuted by circumcision that he was at one time an Israelite, so also you, even if you have separated from the Church or innovated transgression, you are nevertheless refuted by the seal: for you received Baptism in Christ's Church" (18).

Or consider the work of Lactantius, active between the mid third and early fourth century CE. In his Divine Institutes (Institutiones Divinae), in at least one instance, it is not Israel but *Judah* whom Christians have inherited. He refers to Jeremiah 31:32 where God speaks of making a new "testament to the house of Israel and the house of Judah" (4.20).[173] He claims that this text must refer to the New Testament. As a result, it cannot be describing *the Jews* as the house of Judah, "whom he casts off" but instead "us, who have been called by Him out of the Gentiles, and have by adoption succeeded to their place, and are called sons of the Jews" (4.20).[174] That Judah instead of Israel should be used here as Israel so often is elsewhere is, of course, something that exists *in potentia* in a biblical narrative that does end by identifying the Judahites as Israel's final heirs. And here is proof that at least one author could decide to turn that potential into reality, showing just how flexible the redeployment of inherited tradition can be in the hands of an individual author.

Returning to traditions of Israel, however, we can conclude this section by noting that, in addition to those who constructed Christian identity in the guise of a superior, or replacement Israel, compared to the Jewish people, there were also those who used Israel as an ethnic boundary-making concept *against other*

---

[172] Jacobs, "Amphilochius of Iconium." [173] Schaff, *The Complete Works*, 37852.
[174] At one point, he says "[s]ince the inheritance is His heavenly kingdom, it is evident that He does not say that He hates the inheritance itself, but the heirs, who have been ungrateful ... and impious," at another "For that which he said above, that He would make a new testament to the house of Judah, shows that the old testament which was given by Moses was not perfect; but that which was to be given by Christ would be complete. But it is plain that the house of Judah does not signify the Jews, whom He casts off, but us, who have been called by Him out of the Gentiles, and have by adoption succeeded to their place" (Schaff, 37852–53).

Christians. In other words, there were those who claimed they were a truer Israel than other Christian groups, and those who claimed that other groups were too much like Israelites to be Christian.[175] Within the first category, we can certainly count the Donatists, who emerged in response to the Diocletian Persecution, rejecting the authority of those who had tried to appease the Romans by handing over holy books.[176] As Gerda Heydemann observes, they were indeed in the habit of "[p]resenting themselves as the heirs of the biblical Israel" and applying "claims to divine election and special favor" as a result.[177] Peter Brown adds that they believed they "enjoyed a special relationship with God" and they "quote those passages of the prophets of Israel in which they tell of how God had closed His ears to His Chosen People because of their sins."[178]

In the other direction, there were those like the Marcionites. These were the followers of Marcion, a Christian theologian active mainly in the second century CE, perhaps best known in Christian tradition – as Judith Lieu has put it – "for his attempt to sever the God of the Old Testament from the Loving Father of the New, and to deny any consanguinity between Judaism and Christianity."[179] The extent to which Marcion's own views on this subject grew in the telling, sharpened by anti-Marcionite polemic, is hard to ascertain, but the Marcionites at least do seem generally to have rejected the Jewish roots of Christianity.[180] And there were others, both individuals and groups, who virulently attacked what they saw as Judaizing Christians for too great an adherence to the biblical past. There was, for example, the famous crusade of John Chrysostom against the Jews and Judaizers of Antioch, which was so virulent in its anti-Jewish rhetoric that some of his speeches would be used by the Nazis.[181]

At any rate, Simon, in his now dated treatment, already raised the interesting possibility that what I am calling the abiological strategy may actually have developed as much to address these Christian "purists" as the relationship between Christianity and the Jewish people I have focused on. In other words, he argues that the fact that groups like the Marcionites – and the Manichean Christians – were identifying themselves in opposition to Judaizing Christians is part of what inspired Christian authors who saw themselves as part of a mainstream, and Marcionites and Manichaeans as heretical splinter groups,

---

[175] Buell, *Why This New Race*, 3.   [176] Brown, *Augustine of Hippo*, 215.
[177] Heydemann, "People(s) of God?" 41.   [178] Brown, *Augustine of Hippo*, 218.
[179] Lieu, *Image and Reality*, 17.
[180] Lieu, "Marcion's Gospel and the New Testament," 329–34.
[181] Ari Finkelstein argues that among the church fathers, only Ephrem of Nisibis equaled the extremes of Chrysostom's rhetoric (Finkelstein, *The Specter of the Jews*, 141). See, generally, this study and Wilken, *John Chrysostom and the Jews*.

to use Israel language to build boundaries. Certainly, he is correct that there was a "two front" conflict – Jews on one side, "heretical" Christians on the other.[182] And some of the evidence he uses is compelling, including the fact that Justin and Tertullian each wrote dialogues against *both* the Jews and the Marcionites.[183]

Additionally, as Paula Fredriksen notes, not only did Tertullian, at least, "accus[e] his two quite different polemical targets of committing the exact same interpretive error" – that they did not realize that the Hebrew Bible was actually concerned with, and prophetic about, the coming of Jesus – he certainly did employ this view to strengthen the boundaries he was rhetorically building against both.[184] In other words, she argues, he happily "appropriate[d]" Marcion's own critique of the Jews and Judaism against them in order to condemn their error as he saw it, while "assert[ing], against Marcion, the Christian authority of the Jewish books. The more Marcion criticized the Jewish god, the more Tertullian reclaimed that God for his own Christianity by repudiating God's recalcitrant ancient followers."[185]

Meanwhile, both sides of this dynamic are also visible in Augustine's famous *Contra Faustum*, where the Faustus in question is a Manichean Christian leader. Here, Augustine's interlocutor, either a real or literary Faustus, certainly does defend Manichaeism as "the purest form of Christianity" against the Catholicism of Augustine.[186] What he means is precisely that Manichean Christianity had made a full break with the Israelite and Jewish past that influenced other forms of Christianity. Therefore, he regarded Christian efforts to make something out of the Hebrew Bible's prophecies, and to adopt and adapt some of the customs it prescribed, as the province of a kind of "semi-Jew."[187] This discussion, as Fredriksen astutely observes, uses Jews not as they actually were but as part of "*a rhetorical strategy.* They are conjured in order to assist their authors in positioning themselves advantageously within the *agon* of intra-Christian theological dispute."[188] But, as we have amply seen, they could also be conjured to assist the author in positioning themselves advantageously

---

[182] That is, that the desire to articulate a distinction between an emerging mainstream Christianity and groups who "deviate[d] from officially accepted teaching or profess[ed] erroneous opinions" like the Arians, Adoptionists, Monarchianists, and others, was just as important as the growing separation between Christianity and Judaism in leading the Church to an "affirmation of the value of the Old Testament" and ever more explicit acknowledgement of "its debt to the synagogue" (Simon, *Verus Israel*, 96).

[183] Simon, 70.   [184] Fredriksen, *Augustine and the Jews*, 224–25.

[185] Fredriksen, *Augustine and the Jews*, 225.   [186] Fredriksen, *Augustine and the Jews*, 214.

[187] See *Contra Faustum,* 33.3, in Schaff, *The Complete Works*, 8270. See also the discussion in Fredriksen, *Augustine and the Jews*, 218–19.

[188] Fredriksen, *Augustine and the Jews*, 227.

within the *agon* of interfaith dispute *too*. Such is the flexibility of an inherited repertoire of Israel language in actual practice.

Taken together, then, all of these examples clearly illustrate the considerable range of what an individual author might do with an inherited repertoire of traditions for constructing identities. Such an author might use them in a familiar way, but with individual twists that are subtle or not so subtle. Or it may occur to an individual at any moment to do something quite unfamiliar, to decide that the inherited vocabulary elements of Samaritan Israelite or Judahite can do what other authors are using Israel to do. They show that an author, using the same traditions as another, may still choose of their own volition to place ethnic boundaries nearer or farther away, as close to hand as between two Christian groups, or as far as all the children of Abraham or Adam, beyond even Christianity itself. They show that an author can think that the question of who the true Israel is can be mainly a matter of concern in this life, or in the next. And they do indeed show, as well, that when someone engages with the kind of identifying that we call "ethnic," they may describe its formation as a consequence of descent – *or* something else altogether, including shared belief or spiritual identity.

Thus, within this busy context of discourse and counter-discourse, we should understand the abiological strategy as one prominent option for making ethnic boundaries, and we should understand it as a starting point from which many different arguments could proceed. Its abiological character is what makes clear that each of the strategies discussed in this Element are *just* that, strategies, each as valid as the next – which is to say that biological descent is not a *de rigeur* way of doing ethnic business with others, still less the reasonable, intuitive, or more accurate way. It is simply *a* way. And in bringing all of these different ways of identifying as Israel conceptually closer together, we do indeed provide ourselves with a wonderful opportunity to appreciate just how much variety ethnic expression is capable of achieving.

Conclusion

In some ways, the intellectual challenge of understanding ethnicity resembles the challenge of understanding the Babylonian Talmud, one of the first collections I discussed. On the one hand, the finished Talmud is clearly a repository of a good deal of inherited material: of quotations and ideas passed down through the generations. Additionally, in familiar reconstructions of what the Talmud is, the chain stretches even farther back, to laws and traditions entrusted in some way to Moses on Sinai itself, or else, the distillation of the "consistent exegesis" of the written Torah from just as long ago.[189] This more ancient wisdom, the story goes, was plucked from the fires of burning Jerusalem in 70 CE by Yohanan Ben Zakkai, founder of the rabbinic academy at Yavneh, consolidated by Judah the Prince into the Mishnah, and explicated by the rabbinic sages of a handful of later generations in the form of the Gemara. The result, supposedly, is a collection that is much more the *crystallization* of something much older than a meaningful product of the time and place that saw it emerge.[190]

In recent years, however, scholarly understandings of the Babylonian Talmud have diverged considerably from this traditional picture. For one thing, we recognize that, as a practical matter, the timeline is wrong and considerably too early. Significant developments continued to occur well after the fifth century CE.[191] Indeed, Moulie Vidas notes that the Talmud only clearly "began circulating in written copies" in the ninth century, while "in the twelfth century, R. Jacob b. Meir admonished those who changed the texts . . . not just in parts that 'seem like an interpretation,' but in 'the words of the tanna'im and amorai'im themselves.'"[192] In addition, serious questions are now being asked about the relationship between the finished product and early materials, even in contexts that explicitly present themselves as inherited sayings. Simcha Gross, for one, has argued that there is reason to suspect that much of what is presented as ancient wisdom is "reformulations, if not outright creations, of later editorial hands."[193] As a result, the physical production of the Talmud now seems to have taken place later, to have stretched over a longer period of time, and to have been much more dynamic into later centuries than the traditional picture suggests.

Just as important as the practical questions of when and by whom Talmudic texts were written, however, the conceptual understanding of the nature of their production is also undergoing revision. Since the work of David Weiss Halivni, scholarship, broadly, has particularly appreciated anew the importance of the

---

[189] Strack and Stemberger, *Introduction*, 142; Neusner, *Introduction to Rabbinic Literature*, xx.

[190] See, generally, Strack and Stemberger, *Introduction*, 132–44, 192–213.

[191] Strack and Stemberger, *Introduction*, 212–13. They note that "even after the Saboraim had given the Talmud tractates their essential shape, scholars during the transition from the Saboraim to the Geonim (whose eras cannot be clearly delimited) did not shy away from inserting further explanations into the text of BT itself," meaning the Babylonian Talmud. "However, in the middle of the eighth century BT was already regarded as a closed work" (Strack and Stemberger, *Introduction*, 206–7). Even so, they also observe something that is clearly visible to anyone familiar with what the Talmud actually looks like, which is that the text is bracketed by "marginal glosses" from figures like Rashi, active in the eleventh century (Strack and Stemberger, *Introduction*, 223).

[192] Vidas, *Tradition and the Formation of the Talmud*, 208.

[193] Gross, *Babylonian Jews*, 22. He adds that "[t]he redactors were responsible for much of the Talmud as we know it; they compiled earlier opinions into what appears to be linear legal discussions and connected one textual unit to the next. They produced the anonymous Aramaic discursive tissue that holds Talmudic legal discussions and stories together."

anonymous voice that introduces, organizes, arbitrates between, and weighs in on the various discussions, stories, quotes, and rulings that make up the Talmudic text. This voice is called the "Stam," "after the Aramaic *setam*, or 'anonymous,'" and, as Yaakov Elman observes, it constitutes "over half of the total text of the Babylonian Talmud."[194] Halivni argued – reasonably! – that, in addition to the eras of the Tannaim who produced the Mishnah, the Amoraim who produced the Gemaras, and the Saboraim, or "reasoners," who, in the traditional model, gave final shape to the Talmuds, we should allow for an era of "Stammaim," whose work it was to give inherited debates their familiar shape.[195] After all, it is clearly their work that stands as the backbone of the finished collection.

The (conceptual) question, however, is what did the work of these Stammaim consist of? Halivni Weiss's vision was conservative. They limited themselves, he felt, to "reconstruct[ing] the argumentation" of previous ages, passed down orally, "and entrusted ... to transmitters so that it be preserved for future generations."[196] This is not very plausible, and subsequent scholarship has acknowledged as much. Monika Amsler – who argues forcefully that the Talmud should not only be understood as a Late Antique literary production but as a participant in Late Antique genres that appear outside of Jewish circles – has, for example, analogized the operation of the Stammaim to that of a "composer" engaged in the "orchestration of different voices," creating, thereby, their own music.[197] The fact that some of the notes already existed, in this image, would certainly not predetermine the nature of the song. In any case, rather than a model in which the Babylonian Talmud was barely even a product of the era in which it was physically produced, because of how completely its producers relied on what had been done generations before, we should now employ one in which even those Talmudic authors who were working with inherited traditions had a lot of agency about what to make from them. The tradiional vision of deep continuity over time should now be inverted.

When it comes to conventional understandings of ethnicity, the same basic patterns indeed tend to hold. Intellectually, we may be aware that there are modern, or contemporaneous, features to any ethnic construction. But even in scholarship, we sometimes represent ethnic groups, in their essence, as the latest

---

[194] Amsler, *The Babylonian Talmud and Late Antique Book Culture*, 4–5; Elman, "The Babylonian Talmud in Its Historical Context," 19.

[195] See, generally, Halivni, *The Formation of the Babylonian Talmud*, i   [196] Halivni, 4–5.

[197] Amsler, *The Babylonian Talmud*, 29. Overall, she argues that the Babylonian Talmud is "a commentary in form, an encyclopedia in content, and a symposiac work in its literary mode" (Amsler, 16–17).

links in a chain stretching back into the distant past. And acknowledgments of how much can owe to the activity of later inheritors often co-exist with explanations for why the redescriptive potential of this later activity should be essentially discounted, as in Halivni Weiss's work. Indeed, even those who recognize that ethnic constructions can emerge, whole cloth, with little notice are still often caught up in what Jonathan M. Hall called the "sterile debate between ethnic truth and ethnic fiction," which is to say, debates primarily concerned with which ethnic constructions *are* familiar crystallizations of more ancient identity formations.[198] In fact, "Cultural Invention" theory emerged in the 1980s primarily as a way of distinguishing between those that were and those that were not inventions.[199] It was still presumed that "genuine traditions" marked a group out as fundamentally different from those that had been "invented."[200]

In reality, the problem with conventional, conservative models of ethnic inheritance is not that they fail to recognize that, in some cases, the contents of an ethnic identity could be invented, rather than genuine – just as the problem with older models of the Babylonian Talmud is not that they failed to recognize the activity of the Stammaim. In both cases, it is that they denied agency to those who inherit traditions and the inherent fluidity of inheritance in reality, everywhere observed and even when the traditions in question are much more ancient. They hold out simply preserving and passing on as a much more plausible option than it actually is. Today, in scholarship, there is no rescuing the traditional vision of the Babylonian Talmud by imagining the Stammaim as something different from what other heirs of tradition have been and there is no rescuing "real" ethnicities by toting up continuities with the distant past. Very often, constructing ethnicity *is* a matter of making something out of what lies to hand. But we make a mistake when we think the antiquity of the contents, even when it exists, can outweigh the dynamism of any attempt to make them something new.

One way I have tried to make this case, both here and in my previous book, is to point to the lesson provided by the mere existence of this business of making Israels all around the world. Biblical traditions are ancient – but they don't *belong*, in the sense that we imagine the traditions of a cultural group belong to that group, to a great many of the world's Israels. Or perhaps we should say they belong to all of them in approximately equal measure. But if a group can suddenly emerge, creating an identity out of a different set of traditions than

---

[198] Hall, *Ethnic Identity in Greek Antiquity*, 19.
[199] With the pioneering work of Eric Hobsbawm, in Hobsbawm and Ranger, eds., *The Invention of Tradition*. See the discussion in Tobolowsky, *The Myth of the Twelve Tribes of Israel*, 45–50.
[200] Hobsbawm, "Introduction: Inventing Traditions," 7–8.

their biological ancestors did, that is how much change an identity can experience over time. When Gentile Christians construct themselves as an Israel, this is what they are doing, making something from traditions that they were able to access because of their embrace of biblical traditions and not because of who their ancestors were. It may even be, as many scholars now acknowledge, that the Judahites who gave us biblical Israel were up to this too – that their own early ancestors thought of themselves as Judahites *rather than* Israelites.[201]

Another way is to emphasize, as I have emphasized throughout, that the business of making visions of ethnic identity is *inherently* individual. Individuals may try to simply rehearse what has been handed down, or not, but either way, they will be guided by their own individual and idiosyncratic vision of what is important about their inheritance and what its significance is. For this reason, what we have seen throughout is *stunning* variety. Authors engaged in ethnic boundary-making can construct new visions of ethnic identity by telling an old story in a new way, or by reinterpreting it altogether. They can choose to elevate a different old story than the usual and push another to the background. They can make exceptions, and justify exceptions, or explain why exceptions are no exceptions at all. They can claim to have become, spiritually, what their ancestors were not, or to have been literally reborn. They can decide that the essential contents of an ethnicity are fundamentally different from what it seemed to be before.

Thus, here at the end, I reiterate a conclusion reached also by others, such as Buell and Miller: that *the making itself* is what ethnicity is. Ethnicity is not a set of contents, and it is not a strategy. Instead, within a cultural watershed, different contents and strategies are available to greater and lesser degrees, waiting to be *turned into* constructions of ethnicity. How any individual author chooses to navigate a culturally available repertoire and turn it into a vision of the ethnic group depends on many factors, *including* the psychology and intentions of that individual. And more is possible in terms of boundary crossing, invention, and reinvention than we usually acknowledge.

In addition, I want to emphasize once more that the phenomenon of a world full of Israels holds unusual potential for studying ethnicity in two directions. First, it offers a rare opportunity to see what so many different groups do with the *same* traditions to construct the *same* identity. From here we can indeed see how much variety the "same" tradition heritage is capable of expressing for different authors in different contexts. Second, it allows us to see how individuals and groups can move *between* tradition heritages in a way that challenges the notion that part of what defines an ethnic group is the inheritance of a shared

---

[201] Tobolowsky, *The Myth of the Twelve Tribes of Israel*, 11.

repertoire of traditions throughout the generations. Both recognitions should focus our attention away from trying to define "an" ethnic identity and towards treating as definitional the latent potential of a set of ethnic contents to be used in countless acts of boundary-making by countless individuals. In other words, we should define ethnicity as what it does.

Finally, as for defining ethnic identity primarily in terms of traditions of shared descent, it is indeed as Buell and others have argued. Claiming descent is not the sine qua non of ethnicity; it is just one strategy among many. Clearly, if someone you are in competition with claims to be Israel by right of exclusive biological descent, denying that claim is only one way to respond. Another is to claim that descent is an *insufficient* quantity for defining an ethnic group, and another, that it is irrelevant altogether. All of these options exist, and more. The right mind, in the right place, can call them forth.

Bibliography

Adler, Yonatan. *The Origins of Judaism: An Archaeological-Historical Reappraisal*. New Haven, CT: Yale University Press, 2022.

Alon, Gedaliah. "The Origin of the Samaritans in the Halakhic Tradition." In *Jews, Judaism, and the Classical World: Studies in Jewish History in the Times of the Second Temple and Talmud*, translated by J. Abrahams, 354–73. Jerusalem, Israel: Magnes Press, 1977.

Ambrose. *Explanation on 12 Psalms*. Edited by Michael Petschenig and Michaela Zelzer. 64. Corpus Scriptorum Ecclesiasticorum Latinorum, 1999.

Amsler, Monika. *The Babylonian Talmud and Late Antique Book Culture*. Cambridge: Cambridge University Press, 2023.

Anderson, Robert T., and Terry Giles. *Tradition Kept: The Literature of the Samaritans*. Peabody, MA: Hendrickson Publishers, 2005.

Angel, Joseph L. "'Kinsmen' or an 'Alien Race?': Jews and Samaritans from the Hasmoneans to the Mishnah." In *The Samaritans: A Biblical People*, edited by Steven Fine, 53–60. Leiden: Brill, 2022.

Ballentine, Debra. "Foreignization in Ancient Competition." *Journal of Religious Competition in Antiquity* 1, no. 1 (2019): 18–36.

Becker, Adam H., and Annette Yoshiko Reed. *The Ways That Never Parted: Jews and Christians in Late Antiquity and the Early Middle Ages*. Minneapolis, MN: Fortress Press, 2003.

Ben-Eliyahu, Eyal, Yehudah Cohn, and Fergus Millar. *Handbook of Jewish Literature from Late Antiquity*. Oxford: Oxford University Press, 2012.

Bowersock, G. W., Peter Brown, and Oleg Grabar, eds. *Late Antiquity: A Guide to the Postclassical World*. Cambridge, MA: Harvard University Press, 1999.

Brown, Peter. *Augustine of Hippo: A Biography*. Berkeley, CA: University of California Press, 1969.

Late Antiquity. Cambridge, MA: Harvard University Press, 1998.

The World of Late Antiquity: AD 150–750. New York: Norton, 1989.

Brubaker, Rogers. *Ethnicity Without Groups*. Cambridge, MA: Harvard University Press, 2004.

Nationalist Politics and Everyday Ethnicity in a Transylvanian Town. Princeton, NJ: Princeton University Press, 2006.

Bruneau, Phillippe, and Pierre Bordreuil. "Les Israélites de Délos et la juiverie délienne." *Bulletin de correspondance hellénique* 106, no. 1 (1982): 465–504.

Buell, Denise. *Why This New Race: Ethnic Reasoning in Early Christianity*. New York: Columbia University Press, 2005.

Chadwick, Henry. "The Early Church." In *Christianity: Two Thousand Years*, edited by Richard Harries and Mayr-Harting, Henry, 1–20. Oxford: Oxford University Press, 2001.

Chalmers, Matthew. "Samaritans, Biblical Studies, and Ancient Judaism: Recent Trends." *Currents in Biblical Research* 20, no. 1 (October 2021): 28–64.

———. "Viewing Samaritans Jewishly: Josephus, the Samaritans, and the Identification of Israel." *Journal for the Study of Judaism* 51, no. 3 (2020): 339–66.

Chalmers, Matthew J. "The Rise and Fall of a Peripheral People? Samaritans and the Discourse of Late Antique Disaster." *Studies in Late Antiquity* 6, no. 2 (2022): 217–47.

Chapoutot, Johann. *Greeks, Romans, Germans: How the Nazis Usurped Europe's Classical Past*. Translated by Richard R. Nybakken. Berkeley, CA: University of California Press, 2016.

Charlesworth, James H. *Old Testament Pseudepigrapha*. Vol. 2. Garden City: Doubleday and Company, 1985.

Clark, Elizabeth A. *Founding the Fathers: Early Church History and Protestant Professors in Nineteenth-Century America*. Philadelphia, PA: University of Pennsylvania Press, 2011.

Cohen, Rodrigo Laham. *The Jews in Late Antiquity*. New edition. York: Arc Humanities Press, 2018.

Cohen, Shaye J. D. *The Beginnings of Jewishness: Boundaries, Varieties, Uncertainties*. Berkeley, CA: University of California Press, 1999.

Collins, John J. "The Epic of Theodotus and the Hellenism of the Hasmoneans." *The Harvard Theological Review* 73, no. 1/2 (1980): 91–104.

Crane, Oliver Turnbull. *The Samaritan Chronicle or The Book of Joshua, The Son of Nun*. New York: John B. Alden, 1890.

Crouch, Carly L. *The Making of Israel: Cultural Diversity in the Southern Levant and the Formation of Ethnic Identity in Deuteronomy*. Leiden: Brill, 2014.

Crown, Alan D. "Samaritan Literature and Its Manuscripts." *Bulletin of the John Rylands Library* 76, no. 1 (1994): 21–50.

Drake, Susanna. *Slandering the Jew: Sexuality and Difference in Early Christian Texts*. Philadelphia, PA: University of Pennsylvania Press, 2013.

Dunn, Geoffrey D. *Tertullian*. London: Routledge, 2004.

Dušek, Jan. *Aramaic and Hebrew Inscriptions from Mt. Gerizim and Samaria between Antiochus III and Antiochus IV Epiphanes*. Culture and History of the Ancient Near East 54. Leiden: Brill, 2012.

Elman, Yaakov. "The Babylonian Talmud in Its Historical Context." In *Printing the Talmud: From Bomberg to Schottenstein*, edited by Sharon Lieberman Mintz and Gabriel M. Goldstein, 19–27. New York: New York Yeshiva University, 2005.

Epiphanius, Saint, and Frank Williams. *The Panarion of Epiphanius of Salamis. Book I (Sects 1–46)*. 2nd ed., Revised and Expanded. Nag Hammadi and Manichaean Studies, v. 63. Leiden: Brill, 2009.

Eshel, Esther, and Hanan Eshel. "Dating the Samaritan Pentateuch's Compilation in Light of the Qumran Biblical Scrolls." In *Emanuel: Studies in the Hebrew Bible, Septuagint, and Dead Sea Scrolls in Honor of Emanuel Tov*, edited by Shalom M. Paul. Vetus Testamentum Supplement 94. Leiden: Brill, 2003.

Eyl, Jennifer. "'I Myself Am an Israelite': Paul, Authenticity and Authority." *Journal for the Study of the New Testament* 40, no. 2 (December 1, 2017): 148–68.

Feldman, Louis H. *Jew and Gentile in the Ancient World*. Attitudes and Interactions from Alexander to Justinian. Princeton, NJ: Princeton University Press, 1993.

Fine, Steven. "'The Consolation of Souls, the Assurer of Hearts, and the Certainty of Truth': The Abisha Scroll." In *The Samaritans: A Biblical People*, edited by Steven Fine, 15–31. Leiden: Brill, 2022.

Finkelstein, Ari. *The Specter of the Jews: Emperor Julian and the Rhetoric of Ethnicity in Syrian Antioch*. The S. Mark Taper Foundation Imprint in Jewish Studies. Berkeley, CA: University of California Press, 2018.

Fredriksen, Paula. *Augustine and the Jews*. New York: Doubleday, 2008.

Paul: The Pagans' Apostle. New Haven, CT: Yale University Press, 2017.

Fried, Lisbeth S. *Ezra and the Law in History and Tradition*. Columbia, SC: University of South Carolina Press, 2014.

Friedheim, Emmanuel. "Some Notes about the Samaritans and the Rabbinic Class at the Crossroads." In *Samaritans: Past and Present: Current Studies*, edited by Menachem Mor, Friedrich V. Reiterer, and Waltraud Winkler, 193–202. Berlin: De Gruyter, 2010.

Geary, Patrick J. *The Myth of Nations: The Medieval Origins of Europe*. Princeton, NJ: Princeton University Press, 2002.

Graves, Michael. *Biblical Interpretation in the Early Church*. Minneapolis, MN: Fortress Press, 2017.

Gross, Simcha. *Babylonian Jews and Sasanian Imperialism in Late Antiquity*. Cambridge: Cambridge University Press, 2024.

Halivni, David Weiss. *The Formation of the Babylonian Talmud*. Oxford: Oxford University Press, 2013.

Hall, Jonathan M. *Ethnic Identity in Greek Antiquity*. Leiden: Cambridge University Press, 1997.

Harvey, Graham. *The True Israel: Uses of the Names Jew, Hebrew, and Israel in Ancient Jewish and Early Christian Literature*. Leiden: Brill, 2001.

Heydemann, Gerda. "People(s) of God?: Biblical Exegesis and the Language of Community in Late Antique and Early Medieval Europe." In *Meanings of

Community across Medieval Eurasia, edited by Eirik Hovden, Christina Lutter, and Walter Pohl, 27–60. Comparative Approaches. Leiden: Brill, 2016.

Hezser, Catherine. "Introduction." In *The Routledge Handbook of Jews and Judaism in Late Antiquity*, edited by Catherine Hezser, 1–12. London: Routledge, 2024.

Hobsbawm, Eric. "Introduction: Inventing Traditions." In *The Invention of Tradition*, edited by Eric Hobsbawm and Terence Ranger, 1–14. Cambridge; New York: Cambridge University Press, 1983.

Hobsbawm, Eric, and Terence Ranger, eds. *The Invention of Tradition*. Cambridge: Cambridge University Press, 1983.

Hodge, Caroline Johnson. *If Sons, Then Heirs: A Study of Kinship and Ethnicity in the Letters of Paul*. Oxford: Oxford University Press, 2007.

Jacobs, Andrew. "Amphilochius of Iconium, Against Heretics." Accessed June 22, 2023. http://andrewjacobs.org/translations/asceticism.html.

James, Edward. "The Rise and Function of the Concept 'Late Antiquity.'" *Journal of Late Antiquity* 1, no. 1 (2008): 20–30.

Japhet, Sara. "Exile and Restoration in the Book of Chronicles." In *The Crisis of Israelite Religion*, edited by Bob Becking and Marjo C. A. Korpel, 33–44. Leiden: Brill, 1999.

Kartveit, Magnar. *The Origins of the Samaritans*. Vetus Testamentum Supplement 128. Leiden: Brill, 2009.

Knoppers, Gary N. *Jews and Samaritans: The Origins and History of Their Early Relations*. Oxford: Oxford University Press, 2013.

Kok, Michael. "The True Covenant People: Ethnic Reasoning in the Epistle of Barnabas." *Studies in Religion/Sciences Religieuses* 40, no. 1 (March 1, 2011): 81–97.

Kulp, Joshua, and Jason Rogoff. *Reconstructing the Talmud*. New York: Hadar Press, 2016.

Lahire, Bernard. *The Plural Actor*. Translated by David Fernbach. Cambridge: Cambridge University Press, 2011.

Lavee, Moshe. "The Samaritan May Be Included – Another Look at the Samaritan in Talmudic Literature." In *Samaritans: Past and Present*, edited by Menachem Mor and Friedrich V. Reiterer, 147–73. Studia Samaritana 5. Berlin: De Gruyter, 2010.

——— "The 'Tractate' of Conversion—BT Yeb. 46–48 and the Evolution of Conversion Procedure." *European Journal of Jewish Studies* 4, no. 2 (2010): 169–213.

Lieber, Laura S. *Classical Samaritan Poetry*. University Park, PA: Eisenbrauns, 2022.

Lieu, Judith. *Christian Identity in the Jewish and Graeco-Roman World.* Oxford: Oxford University Press, 2004.

Image and Reality: The Jews in the World of the Christians in the Second Century. London: Bloomsbury, 2003.

"Marcion's Gospel and the New Testament: Catalyst or Consequence?" *New Testament Studies* 63, no. 2 (April 2017): 329–34.

Malkin, Irad. *The Returns of Odysseus.* Berkeley, CA: University of California Press, 1998.

Martyr, Justin. *Dialogue with Trypho (Selections from the Fathers of the Church, Volume 3).* Edited by Michael Slusser. Translated by Thomas B. Falls. Washington, DC: Catholic University of America Press, 2003.

Miller, James C. "Ethnicity and the Hebrew Bible: Problems and Prospects." *Currents in Biblical Research* 6, no. 2 (2008): 170–213.

Neusner, Jacob. *Introduction to Rabbinic Literature.* Anchor Bible Reference Library. New York: Doubleday, 1994.

Judaism and Its Social Metaphors: Israel in the History of Jewish Thought. Cambridge: Cambridge University Press, 1989.

Niehoff, Maren R. "Circumcision as a Marker of Identity: Philo, Origen and the Rabbis on Gen 17: 1–14." *Jewish Studies Quarterly* 10, no. 2 (2003): 89–123.

Nodet, Etienne. *The Samaritans.* London: Bloomsbury, 2023.

Novenson, Matthew V. *Paul and Judaism at the End of History.* Cambridge: Cambridge University Press, 2024.

Origen, and Henry Chadwick. *Origen: Contra Celsum.* Cambridge: Cambridge University Press, 1980.

Pummer, Reinhard. *The Samaritans: A Profile.* Grand Rapids, MI: Eerdmans, 2016.

Rebillard, Eric. "Material Culture and Religious Identity in Late Antiquity." In *A Companion to the Archaeology of Religion in the Ancient World*, edited by Rubina Raja and Jörg Rüpke, 425–36. Chichester: Wiley Blackwell, 2015.

Rhodes, James N. "The Two Ways Tradition in the 'Epistle of Barnabas:' Revisiting an Old Question." *The Catholic Biblical Quarterly* 73, no. 4 (2011): 797–816.

Roshwald, Mordecai. "Marginal Jewish Sects in Israel (II)." *International Journal of Middle East Studies* 4, no. 3 (1973): 328–54.

Rubenson, Samuel. *The Letters of St. Antony: Monasticism and the Making of a Saint.* Minneapolis, MN: Fortress Press, 1995.

Runia, David T. "Clement of Alexandria and the Philonic Doctrine of the Divine Power(s)." *Vigiliae Christianae* 58, no. 3 (2004): 256–76.

Rutgers, Leonard Victor. "Archaeological Evidence for the Interaction of Jews and Non-Jews in Late Antiquity." *American Journal of Archaeology* 96, no. 1 (1992): 101–18.

Schaff, Philip, ed. *The Complete Works of the Church Fathers: A Total of 64 Authors, and over 2,500 Works of the Early Christian Church*. Toronto: Public Domain, 2016.

Schenker, Adrian. "Le Seigneur Choisira-t-Il Le Lieu de Son Nom Ou l'a-t-Il Choisi? L'apport de La Bible Grecque Ancienne á l'histoire Du Texte Samaritain et Massorétique." In *Scripture in Transition: Essays on Septuagint, Hebrew Bible, and Dead Sea Scrolls in Honour of Raija Sollamo*, edited by Anssi Voitila and Jutta Jokiranta, 339–51. Leiden: Brill, 2008.

Schick, Shana Strauch, and Steven Fine. "'Do You Have an Onion?': Rabbis and Samaritans in Late Antiquity." In *The Samaritans: A Biblical People*, edited by Steven Fine, 73–80. Leiden: Brill, 2022.

Schiffman, Lawrence H. "The Samaritans in Tannaitic Halakhah." *The Jewish Quarterly Review* 75, no. 4 (1985): 323–50.

Schorch, Stefan. "A Critical Editio Maior of the Samaritan Pentateuch: State of Research, Principles, and Problems." *Hebrew Bible and Ancient Israel* 2 (2013): 1–21.

"The Construction of Samari(t)an Identity from the Inside and the Outside." In *Between Cooperation and Hostility: Multiple Identities in Ancient Judaism and the Interaction with Foreign Powers*, edited by Rainer Albertz and Jakob Wöhrle, 135–50. Göttingen: Vandenhoeck & Ruprecht, 2013.

"'Woe to Those Who Exchanged the Truth for a Lie, When They Choose for Themselves a Different Place': Samaritan Perspectives on the Samaritan-Jewish Split." In *The Samaritans: A Biblical People*, edited by Steven Fine, 41–52. Leiden: Brill, 2022.

Schott, Jeremy M. *Christianity, Empire, and the Making of Religion in Late Antiquity*. Philadelphia, PA: University of Pennsylvania Press, 2008.

Schwartz, Seth. "How Many Judaisms Were There?: A Critique of Neusner and Smith on Definition and Mason and Boyarin on Categorization." *Journal of Ancient Judaism* 2, no. 2 (2011): 208–38.

Shepardson, Christine. "Christianity Emerges in the Era of Late Antiquity." *Entangling Web: The Fractious Story of Christianity in Europe* 4 (2024): 1.

Siker, Jeffrey S. *Disinheriting the Jews: Abraham in Early Christian Controversy*. Louisville, KY: Westminster John Knox, 1991.

Simon, Marcel. *Verus Israel: A Study of the Relations between Christians and Jews in the Roman Empire, AD 135–425*. Oxford: The Littman Library of Jewish Civilization, 2009.

Smith, Anthony D. *The Ethnic Origins of Nations*. Oxford: Basil Blackwell, 1986.

Staples, Jason A. *Paul and the Resurrection of Israel: Jews, Former Gentiles, Israelites*. Cambridge: Cambridge University Press, 2023.

———. *The Idea of Israel in Second Temple Judaism: A New Theory of People, Exile, and Israelite Identity*. Cambridge: Cambridge University Press, 2021.

Stemberger, Günter. "Non-Rabbinic Literature." In *Judaism in Late Antiquity 1. The Literary and Archaeological Sources*, edited by Jacob Neusner, 11–39. Leiden: Brill, 1994.

Stern, Karen B. *Writing on the Wall: Graffiti and the Forgotten Jews of Antiquity*. Princeton, NJ: Princeton University Press, 2018.

Stoler, Ann Laura. "Racial Histories and Their Regimes of Truth." *Political Power and Social Theory* 11, no. 1 (1997): 183–206.

Strack, Hermann L., and Günter Stemberger. *Introduction to the Talmud and Midrash*. Translated by Markus Bockmuehl. Edinburgh, Scotland: T & T Clark, 1991.

Strassfeld, Max K. *Trans Talmud: Androgynes and Eunuchs in Rabbinic Literature*. Berkeley, CA: University of California Press, 2023.

Tal, Abraham. *Tibat Marqe: The Ark of Marqe*. Berlin: De Gruyter, 2019.

Thiessen, Matthew. *A Jewish Paul: The Messiah's Herald to the Gentiles*. Grand Rapids, MI: Baker Books, 2023.

Tobolowsky, Andrew. *The Myth of the Twelve Tribes of Israel: New Identities Across Time and Space*. Cambridge: Cambridge University Press, 2022.

———. "The Thor Movies and the 'Available Myth': Mythic Reinvention in Marvel Movies." In *Theology and the Marvel Universe*, edited by Gregory Stevenson 173–86. Lanham, MD: Lexington Books, 2020.

Tsedaka, Benyamim. "Families." *Israelite Samaritan Information Institute* (blog), n.d. www.israelite-samaritans.com/about-israelite-samaritans/families/.

Vidas, Moulie. *Tradition and the Formation of the Talmud*. Princeton, NJ: Princeton University Press, 2016.

Weingart, Kristin. "What Makes an Israelite an Israelite? Judean Perspectives on the Samarians in the Persian Period." *Journal for the Study of the Old Testament* 42, no. 2 (2017): 155–75.

White, L. Michael. "The Delos Synagogue Revisited: Recent Fieldwork in the Graeco-Roman Diaspora." *Harvard Theological Review* 80, no. 2 (1987): 133–60.

Wilken, Robert L. *John Chrysostom and the Jews: Rhetoric and Reality in the Late 4th Century*. Wipf and Stock Publishers, 2004.

Wimmer, Andreas. "Herder's Heritage and the Boundary-Making Approach: Studying Ethnicity in Immigrant Societies." *Sociological Theory* 27, no. 3 (2009): 244–70.

———. "The Making and Unmaking of Ethnic Boundaries: A Multilevel Process Theory." *American Journal of Sociology* 113, no. 4 (2008): 970–1022.

Wollenberg, Rebecca Scharbach. *The Closed Book: How the Rabbis Taught the Jews (Not) to Read the Bible*. Princeton, NJ: Princeton University Press, 2023.

Yerushalmi, Yosef Hayim. *Zakhor: Jewish History and Jewish Memory*. Seattle, WA: University of Washington Press, 1996.

Cambridge Elements

Religion in Late Antiquity

Andrew S. Jacobs
Harvard Divinity School

Andrew S. Jacobs is Senior Fellow at the Center for the Study of World Religions at Harvard Divinity School. He has taught at the University of California, Riverside, Scripps College, and Harvard Divinity School and is the author of *Remains of the Jews: The Holy Land and Christian Empire in Late Antiquity; Christ Circumcised: A Study in Early Christian History and Difference; and Epiphanius of Cyprus: A Cultural Biography of Late Antiquity*. He has co-edited *Christianity in Late Antiquity, 300–450 C.E.: A Reader* and *Garb of Being: Embodiment and the Pursuit of Asceticism in Late Ancient Christianity*.

Editorial Board
Krista Dalton, *Kenyon College*
Heidi Marx, *University of Manitoba*
Ellen Muehlberger, *University of Michigan*
Michael Pregill, *Los Angeles, California*
Kristina Sessa, *Ohio State University*
Stephen J. Shoemaker, *University of Oregon*

About the Series

This series brings a holistic and comparative approach to religious belief and practice from 100–800 C.E. throughout the Mediterranean and Near East. Volumes will explore the key themes that characterize religion in late antiquity and will often cross traditional disciplinary lines. The series will include contributions from classical studies, Early Christianity, Judaism, and Islam, among other fields.

Cambridge Elements ☰

Religion in Late Antiquity

Elements in the Series

Theory, History, and the Study of Religion in Late Antiquity: Speculative Worlds
Maia Kotrosits

Monasticism and the City in Late Antiquity and the Early Middle Ages
Mateusz Fafinski and Jakob Riemenschneider

Israel and Its Heirs in Late Antiquity
Andrew Tobolowsky

A full series listing is available at: www.cambridge.org/ELAN

For EU product safety concerns, contact us at Calle de José Abascal, 56–1°, 28003 Madrid, Spain or eugpsr@cambridge.org.

www.ingramcontent.com/pod-product-compliance
Lightning Source LLC
LaVergne TN
LVHW020352260326
834688LV00045B/1674